PRESENTING SCOTLAND'S STORY

PRESENTING SCOTLAND'S STORY

Edited by Timothy Ambrose

Her Majesty's Stationery Office
Edinburgh

The Scottish Museums Council is an independent company, principally funded by the Secretary of State for Scotland. The Council's purpose is to improve the quality of local museum and gallery provision in Scotland. This it endeavours to do by providing a wide range of advice, services and financial assistance to its membership in the private and public sectors.

Scottish Museums Council
County House
20-22 Torphichen Street
Edinburgh
EH3 8JB

Crown Copyright 1989
First published 1989

ISBN 0 11 493498 3

PREFACE

Our past has never been so popular. Nor has it to date played so important a role in the leisure and tourism economy. This volume of papers, given at a Scottish Museums Council Conference in November 1988, explores the variety of ways in which the past is being presented to public audiences. New and exciting approaches and techniques in presentation are challenging traditional methods and providing both educational and entertaining experiences for rapidly growing audiences. At the same time, however, fierce debate is taking place in professional circles on the relative merits of new and traditional methodologies. In particular increasing attention is being focussed on the quality of research and the socio-political nature of the historical interpretation which lie behind for example some of the new 'heritage' developments being established in different parts of Scotland and the United Kingdom. These papers reflect that debate, and demonstrate how those charged with the responsibility for presenting Scotland's rich and varied story to present and future audiences continue to question and consider the role and purpose of history in all its forms in the context of changing political ideology.

Museums with their emphasis on interpreting material culture are at the forefront of this process.

But they are not alone, and as this volume shows there are many other equally important ways in which the complex story of the nation is being told – through words and music, buildings and landscapes, drama and film. It is this overall diversity of approach which makes the effective and accurate presentation of Scotland's past such a challenge for the future.

I should like to acknowledge most warmly on behalf of the Scottish Museums Council the support of the various contributors to this volume. In addition I am most grateful to my former assistant Margaret Greeves for her substantial and painstaking work in preparing typescripts and carrying out the administrative work for the publication. Our thanks also go to Geoff Bedford, Director of HMSO Scotland and to Caroline Croyle for her design and layout of the volume. The Conference on which this publication is based was generously supported by the Sunday Mail and the Maxwell Magazine Publishing Ltd.

Timothy Ambrose

Edinburgh,
1st March 1989.

PRESENTING·SCOTLAND'S·STORY

CONTENTS

Preface *Timothy Ambrose*	5
Introduction *Trevor Clark*	9
New Approaches in Presentation? *Don Aldridge*	13
History in the Museum – and out of it *Gaynor Kavanagh*	27
Peopling the Past – the Future of Heritage Presentation *Anthony Gaynor*	39
The National Trust for Scotland – Presenting Scotland's Historic Houses *David Learmont*	47
The Work of the Historic Buildings and Monuments Directorate *David Connelly*	55
Scotland's History in the National Museums of Scotland *Robert Anderson*	65
Scotland's History at the National Galleries *Timothy Clifford*	75
The Drama of Scotland's History *Liz Lochhead*	83
De-picting Scotland: Film, Myth and Scotland's Story *John Caughie*	91

INTRODUCTION

Trevor Clark

Trevor Clark CBE, LVO, was Chairman of the Scottish Museums Council 1981-1984, and was elected again to this position in 1987. He is a former overseas administrator, health board member and Edinburgh City Councillor, and a former Trustee of the National Museums of Scotland. He is a member of the Committee of Area Museums Councils, a member of the Museums Association, and a non-practising barrister.

I suppose that practically the last Westerner to have a broad command of the whole span of the human knowledge that was available to his contemporaries was Isaac Newton. However, we Scots like to think that a century later, during the Age of Enlightenment, a goodly show of folk might have paraded who could make a stab at being omniscient. Our Humes and Smiths, Cockburns and Scotts, enjoyed self-confident intellectual independence, without fluttering gonfalons of embarrassment or arrogance.

Nowadays outsiders see us as more self-conscious about our national qualities, sometimes less attractive in our pride. So much so that our rivals and detractors find it too easy to charge us with chauvinism and self-satisfaction on the one hand, whingeing and endless self-pity on the other. We've got to do something sensible about this, in an age when the whole concept of the nation-state is coming into question. If the barmier barriers are going to fall, perhaps museums and galleries can do their bit of shoving.

It's not enough to get rid of the Scotch Myths of haggis, tartan, whisky and Harry Lauder. As a matter of fact, haggis is a splendid tasty dish (and rather good against heart disease), a kilt's the most comfortable men's dress yet devised for a temperate climate, whiskies make as rewarding a study as good wine (and at more times of the day), while Sir Harry sang some top class popular songs. Some bonnie wee babies can go out with the Tourist Board bath water.

Never mind these superficialities, it's our essential inherited culture that matters. I agree, but be careful. While electronic or jet-propelled communications were shrinking the world down to a global village, we were being persuaded by a generation of sociolinguistic students to see black magic in the power of words. Words were supposed to shape our thoughts; our intelligence didn't control our language. So we have become shy of using familiar shorthand expressions, for fear of distressing someone with a single or very special interest. Spines shiver at 'Tribe', 'Civilisation', 'Man', 'Primitive', even at 'Breeding' or 'Merit'. Granted, it's only good manners (or is that élitist?) to try not to humiliate or irritate people who have some minority difference or disadvantage. But it's equally incumbent on us all, including minority Scotsmen, to remember that one mark of – let me use one of the unfashionable words – 'civilised' persons is the ability to laugh, with others, at themselves. That is why there should always be a small but proper place for Burns Nicht speeches about cromaches, meenisters and shaggy bulls amang the heather, banging saxpences, puffers and Mary Rose's island, some dreamworld of Paw Broon's where we can put our tongues in our cheeks. If we take ourselves too seriously and pedantically all the time, there's little hope that foreigners or neighbours will ever treat us as mature.

The truly great divide in our nation's society is not that carved by geography, or by class, or by income. It is a new one, between those with the self-confidence and the respect for others to be independent but tolerant thinkers, and those with the humourless introspection (it's almost litigious, and certainly bigoted) who see themselves as 'intellectuals', and give intellect a bad name. The former, the wiser, have inherited something broadminded from an earlier liberal system, and they shake their heads sadly at our national 'Letters to the Editor' columns; the latter, too clever for their own good, seem to want every educative process to be a machine tool for introverted social engineering, and they write most of the bilious Letters to our Editors, who print them.

Well, it's genius to know that there's always something new to learn, and it's ignorance to be a know-all. There is no doubt that, whether it's performed from the pulpit or through editorialising in the media, in the classroom or in the lecture hall, teaching is at the heart of our nation's cultural health and of its sickness. Our genes and much of our environment are fixed. Of course the later social anthropologists have given us new uses for that other embarrassing expression, 'Culture', and as more groups take it over, its meaning becomes fuzzier. Not so long ago a 'cultured' person was defined in good Edinburgh-published dictionaries as one who was 'improved by education and training'. The clear implications were that if you were to acquire culture, you had to work at it; and that not only did it not come free like air, but there was a progression up levels of excellence as you went on improving yourself. That conflicts with much received opinion of to-day, where your culture is doing what comes naturally (and if it is unnatural, it is chic).

There's one reaction to our perceived self-doubt going the rounds at the moment, revolving on the belief that, deliberately or by default, Scotland is being Englished. Let me ask a question or two.

Why are Scotsmen so well received when they leave Scotland to make their individual fortunes? (It used to be as missionaries, traders, administrators, bankers, ambassadors, engineers, doctors, seamen, traders, foresters – there may not be so many openings abroad for some of that list now, but there are hi-tech substitutes.)

Why do so few foreigners recognise Scotland as the nursery of geology, of post-Arab scientific medicine, of the electro-magnetic theories underpinning modern physics, of mechanical communications, of political economy, and of the sole surviving competitive sport without bad manners?

Could it be true that all the brilliant weans in that nursery learnt Greek and Latin under the tawse?

What can we attribute in our lifestyle to our terrible climate and our excess of infertile and inhospitable terrain?

Have any of our finest creative artists and musicians (most of whom seem to be modern) started without first making an original reinterpretation of the work of another land?

Is our fundamentally Roman Scots Law more sympathetic with Napoleon's Code than with the common law of Blackstone and Denning?

Are our poor really comparatively poorer than the Third World's poor, or are they just more miserable?

I did not expect any of our contributors to answer these directly, although their different perspectives offer a shifting signpost of avenues to follow (and stones to upturn). One or two disagree strongly with my earlier words of caution, because we breathe the air of freedom together. Much of Scotland's Story, like any people's heritage, is not easily presented in scholarly and truthful dimensions by galleries and museums, particularly if we restrict it to our cherished local doctrines of law, education and Protestant worship: but it can be done, at various degrees of competence, talent and genius. What I believe with some tempered passion is that a small nation, with the population of Hong Kong, must make unique efforts if it is to be noticed favourably in the world; and that it will fail, unless it tries to understand the span of knowledge now shared by the vaster world, that once embraced its wandering weans and now takes for granted what they were first to learn, with sedulous pain, in its nursery. Hong Kong has been noticed, because it is not ashamed to be part of that vast world and to exchange sweat and design for value and virtue. Our story can only now be convincingly presented as one of what we once gave the world, and of what we received back, and what we have since done with that dividend. The same is equally true for the tellers of England's story, and of America's and of Japan's and of Australia's.

When I hear a Chinese child with an Edinburgh accent and a Pakistani child with a Glasgow accent, I perceive the story of Scotland's culture and civilisation as it really is, and like the first generation Polish immigrant who is an acclaimed scholar of Gaeldom, I can't wait to see them all wanting to wear kilts for the right reason. So if an English flavour is added to our inherited highland and lowland mix of Picts, Scots, Romans, Norwegians, Danes, Spaniards, Romany tinkers, Punjabi pedlars and who knows who else, have no fear that we can't absorb it. We'll change, of course, as we always have changed whenever our past culture developed through broad education and training and travel. So will everyone else, and in order to understand and tell our present story to the wider world, we have to link our past geology and biology and crafts and customs and manufactures and science and rituals and prejudices to the wider world of which we have always been part, and to which more of us are now less reluctantly reaching out, as brothers and sisters anxious to share our good things.

In that broader two-way educational purpose our museums can do so much for our visitors and ourselves, taking the world as our oyster. I believe that this colloquium, published during the Scottish Museums Council's Silver Jubilee in Museums Year, should make us all open our eyes and ears at least as widely as our mouths in the quest for a renewed Enlightenment.

Presentation vs Interpretation. How the ship of interpretation was blown off course in the tempest: some Philosophical thoughts.

NEW APPROACHES IN PRESENTATION

Don Aldridge

Don Aldridge, Interpretive Planner, established the interpretive planning system while working for the Countryside Commission for Scotland. He served on the Council of Europe 1975-1981. He is working on a number of major interpretive studies for UK and European government agencies. His many publications include the Monster Book of Environmental Education (1981) and The Principles and Practice of Interpretive Planning (1975).

This paper is given by a consultant who has descended from the top of his penitential column, like the 4th century St. Symeon, to warn you all of a terrible new plague.

Looking first at the definition of environmental interpretation: 'the art of explaining the significance of a place to the visitors who come there, in order to increase their enjoyment and their desire to conserve that site,' *(Aldridge 1972)*,

and then examining the definition of museum interpretation:
'an activity which responsibly explains and/or displays a collection in such a personalised manner as to make its background, significance, meaning and qualities appealing and relevant to the various museum publics,' *(Dunn 1977)*,

and applying these definitions to what we see passing for interpretation today, should convince us that we are speaking in diverse tongues. The terms: museum, visitor centre and heritage centre are being used dangerously, with abandon even; they need closer scrutiny, *(Aldridge 1975)*. Just as a sane system of planning interpretation was beginning to be accepted in Scotland a dreadful disease broke out in a neighbouring country. This now threatens to sweep the length and breadth of Scotland with the most dire consequences for museums and visitor centres alike. There are rumours that even ranger services have been afflicted.

The first symptoms of the plague were recognised when those hitherto quiet and sober administrators who dispense taxpayer's money in the field of environmental and museum interpretation were suddenly unable to distinguish between PRESENTATION and INTERPRETATION. They reverted to childhood behaviour patterns in their search for new exciting, dynamic, enterprising, innovative and (above-all) FUN PRESENTATION MEDIA. Soon they could be seen diving head first into the toy cupboards of interpretation from which some have had to be rescued, still screaming 'I want! I want!'

Not content to use what we thought were the well-established principles of media selection to plan the communication process in museums and in visitor centres, the afflicted ones have set their sights on what they call new media. In the 1960s it was lapse dissolve slide shows; it was back-illuminated copy in reverse (white lettering on black); and it was so-called participatory devices (like turning the handles of querns for some reason) . . . not to be confused with true participation. In the 1970s it was 64-screen multi-media Mega AV Shows and little green holograms with nearly invisible laser beams, very expensive, full of potential but somehow never able to deliver very much.

Now it is costumed guide performers creating pseudo-events to ensure repeat visits from the punters. It is manufactured history which makes the ordinary seem extraordinary, hyping up a theme, so that it fails to communicate the value of history, and devalues everywhere else . . . quite apart from redistributing the available funds in a way that many readers will doubtless question. Add to this the so-called inter-active videos, chariots taking us for a ride . . . backwards! A new generation of visitors to archaeological sites may find them boring because they lack this 'well-researched' fantasy!

The belief that we must all follow the media mode of the moment threatens to trivialise what we are doing. Beware of the pseudo-scientific half-truth: the claim that people will not look at flatwork and that visitors do not read nowadays. (There are certain conditions in which these things may be true but there are other conditions in which they are not true.) I believe that we could be on the very brink of trivialising Scotland's Story and the idea of a single Scottish Heritage Centre might be one of the likely end-products. Am I being fuddy-duddy — surely it would all be harmless fun wouldn't it? Making a local plan of interpretation for a site must have regard for what happened at that place and so the selection process is disciplined. But suppose that instead of interpreting one place like Lismore, or one theme like the Scottishness of Scottish Samplers as documents that can tell a story about socio-economic conditions in Scotland . . . we were to tell Scotland's story in one centre; what a great pudding that would be!

If you put the emphasis not on interpretation of sites or collections but upon CENTRES then you have opened the door to something quite different, although you will probably borrow the thought processes of site and museum interpreters to justify it. Like the much abused word 'theme'. The Heritage Centre Disease employs a lethal combination of narcissistic selection of themes coupled with a failure to identify the significance of places, or events, or regions, because the wrong things are researched or they are not researched in sufficient depth. The word theme in interpretation shouldn't apply to a subject discipline (eg geology, geomorphology, ecology, social history) because these disciplines are the tools that discover the evidence. It is the inter-relationships which reveal site significance hence themes should be abstract and should also be specific to the one site. Choosing subject disciplines as themes can produce duplication as we have already seen in 'Scottish Red Deer/Caledonian Pine Forest Ecology/Whisky Distilling/Granny's Croft House/Jacobites/Clans/Regiments' . . . of course they aren't all identical but some are more identical than others!

I can hear you cry: what about a central computerised orientation centre pointing to the best Tambour embroidery and the best Ayrshire Whitework, the best Lewisian gneiss exposure, the best Jacobite banner, or the best interpretation within a certain radius? In August 1988 at great personal risk, I visited the country where the Heritage Centre Disease originated and took part in a summer school. Although most of the proceedings were conducted by the sufferers themselves (many of them in the most advanced stages of the affliction) it was nevertheless possible to see a way forward. In order to explain how this might hold out some hopes for the future of

Scotland and Scotland's Story it is necessary to give a blow by blow account of the disease which has replaced the well-established practice of interpretive planning.

There followed an illustrated account in the form of a one hundred foot long cartoon in glorious technicolour. We illustrate it here with a few small priceless shards of a monochrome version which was procured by the Ministry of Perfidious Contracts and Apathy from the artist.
(Aldridge,1989).

Bibliography:
Aldridge, D. (1972) Upgrading Interpretation/National Park Centennial Conference 1972 in *Second World Conference on National Parks: Yellowstone,* US National Parks Service and IUCN.
Dunn, J. R. (1977), Museum Interpretation and Education: the Need for a Definition, *Canadian Museums Gazette, 10 (1).*
Aldridge, D. (1975) Principles of Countryside Interpretation and Interpretive Planning, *HMSO for Countryside Commissions, 1975.*
Aldridge, D. (1989) *How the Ship of Interpretation was blown off course in the Tempest: Some Philosophical Thoughts (in forthcoming* Heritage Interpretation: The Natural and Built Environment, *publisher Belhaven Press, Pinters Group, Floral Street,Covent Garden, London. Autumn 1989.)*

The Good Ship Interpretation sank off the Warwickshire coast with terrible loss to this country,

hardly anyone noticed the incident probably because it occurred at the junction of the M5 and M6.

Trinculo who is not an interpreter but a real fun person immediately made replicas of The Good Ship:

it is wonderful to report that his work obtained the most marvellous sponsorship.

Prince Ferdinand who does not believe in interpretive planning fell madly in love with himself

and with his own colour slides but he created some great medieval participatory livid history.

The subsidised consultant Prospero also recreated The Good Ship Interpretation but in his own image

he introduced holograms of black pudding dancers & Anne Cutaway cottages for the kids to make.

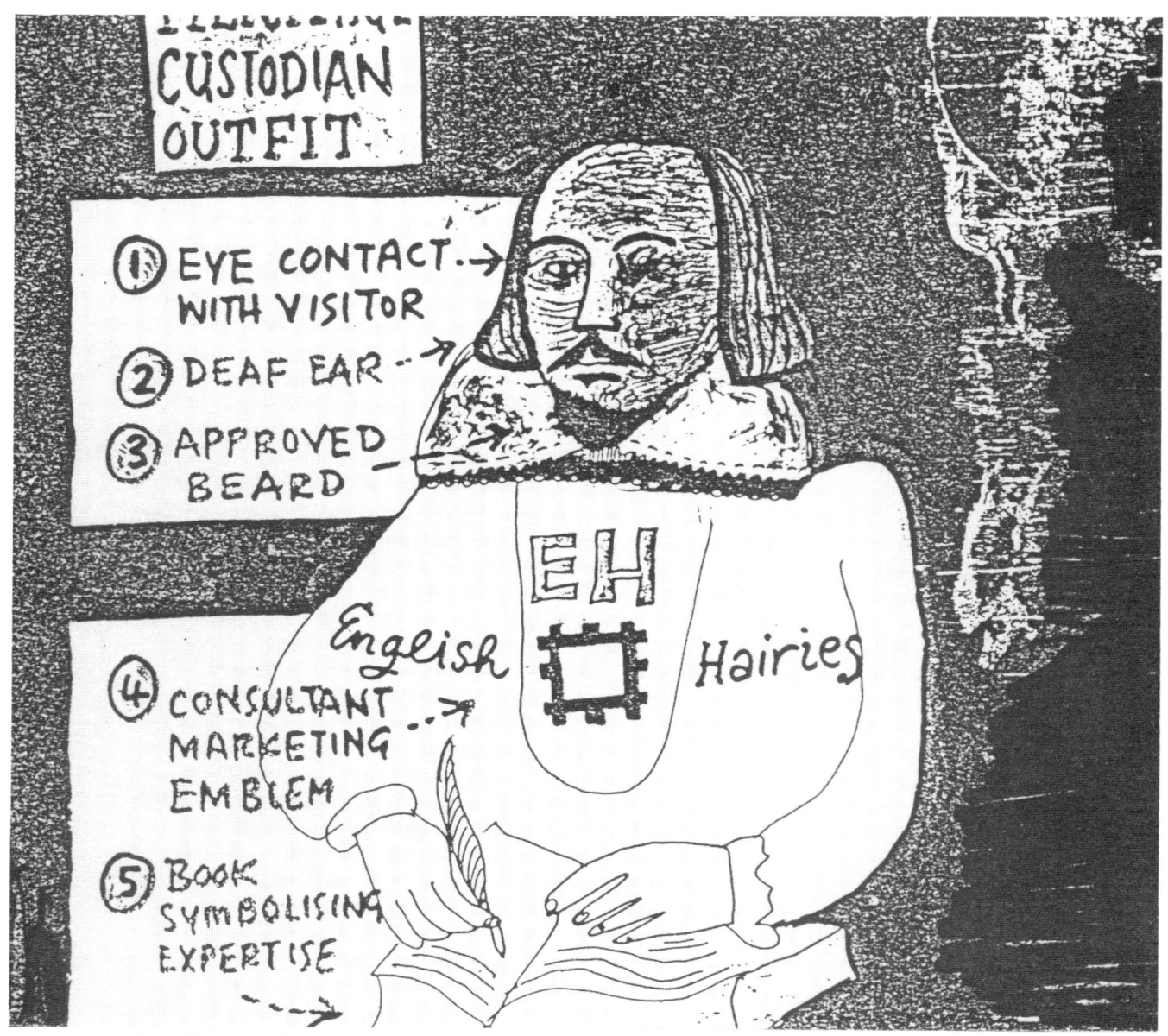
Prospero put on the new heritage uniform while Trinculo launched his Grand Masque of Magical Innovative Fun

with critical mass – bums on seats – guaranteed repeat visits – the video encapsulated white knuckle ride type of interpretation which floats over surfaces without wearing them out or coming to grips with reality.

A display of loosely connected objects and their labels. Here interpretation depends upon the memories and imagination of the visitors.

HISTORY IN THE MUSEUM — AND OUT OF IT

Gaynor Kavanagh

Gaynor Kavanagh has been a lecturer in the Department of Museum Studies at the University of Leicester since 1980. Her research has included a detailed study of museums during the Great War. Her book on history curatorship, theory and practice, for the Leicester Museum Studies Series will be published in the Spring of 1990.

This paper is not about 'Presenting Scotland's Story' and there are three reasons for this. Firstly, I believe there is no form of imperialism more insidious than that of the intellect. Scotland does not need people from organizations outside its boundaries telling it how to cast its own narrative. If it did, then it would not be 'Scotland's Story' at all, but someone else's, saturated with their values and ideas. As I am not a Scot, I shall leave you to make your own stories. Secondly, I have always associated stories with fiction, that is with make-believe, myth, tales and legends. I counter balance this with the idea of history which I associate with facts, methodological records of human experiences, and the interpretation of evidence. Thirdly, whether considering a story or a history, Scotland surely has more than one. Indeed it is in the tension between the different forms of narratives, whether from academics, rembrancers, participants, curators, or commercial 'imagineers', that essential truths about ourselves are found.

Neither stories nor histories come to us innocently, in a moment of intellectual purity. Both are constructions of the way the world is viewed and, although ostensibly about the past, are capable of saying much about present day preoccupations. The strong and recurrent presence of both factual and fictional images in our lives would seem to suggest that we need or are purposefully given both. Whether to keep reality at bay, smooth out discomforting truths, help us cope with or accede to the present, stories and histories are at hand to service our needs.

Our understanding of the past is a collage of narratives and images from many sources including our families, pulp fiction, television drama, history lessons in school, and our ever-lengthening personal histories. In the midst of this stand historians, in the ranks of which are professional historians operating as museum curators. Their responsibilities are quite clear: they must maintain and enlarge our *critical* understanding of the past and present, through the carefully considered use of original evidence. In this task, historians must remain faithful to the essentially anti-authoritarian nature of history studies if they are to strip away the myths and offer ideas and information about the past which have hitherto eluded us. A willingness to question equips historians and not least history curators with a methodological approach that challenges received truths and opens new areas of knowledge. In an era when compassion and criticism appear to have gone out of fashion in the face of a dominant political climate called the New Realism, historians and not least history museums have a vital role to play in keeping some form of perspective on our past and present experiences.

I would like to consider here the role and purpose of history museums in what has become a 'competitive market', the exhibition as historiography and some of the ways forward for re-presenting histories in the medium we call the museum.

The History Museum and History Curatorship
In the last ten years the language of museum practice has been enlarged to accommodate the words 'community', 'heritage', and 'enterprise'. Dealing in notions that are not new to the curatorial profession, these words signify considerable change in attitudes towards and within history museums. But such change is more complex than may appear at first glance. We are in fact witnessing a polarization between the commercialization of a commodity known as 'heritage' and the socialization of an intellectual tradition called 'history'. In general terms, such is the force of this polarization that the ground between the two extremes has become fractured, even fragmented, as museums are pushed and pulled in both directions by competing demands. Clearly, this sense of near rupture occurs in a context where the purpose and worth of history, and by extension history museums, is in transition. Witness, for instance debates in recent years about how history should be taught in schools.

The pull of quick turn-over, mass-appeal, heritage packaging threatens to erode ideas of balance and depth in museum programmes and, more worryingly, to under-cut the place of collections, continued research and acquisition in museums' affairs. The rush for marketable images risks tossing to one side essential facts about history museums and curatorship. The most important of these is the high level of academic and professional training and skills necessary to engage in professional museum work. Without these, curatorship is not equipped to fulfil satisfactorily the potential of the museum in modern life. History curatorship is a highly specialized, professional occupation. It is centred on the gathering, care and explanation of a range of material and aural evidence relating to human activity and experience. Indeed it is in what Marc Bloch called 'the struggle with evidence', with the understanding of sources, which in the case of museums comes in all possible forms, that differences between the professional and the amateur are found. This is as true of museums as it is of other historiographic media. Professional curatorship is the most valuable ingredient that any museum can have. It should be the best defence possible against gloss, surface issues, superficiality, myth and nonsense.

As a medium for recording and discussing the past, the history museum itself has been radically under-estimated. Even though the long and short term purposes of history museums are well established in theory, they need to be re-stated, often and publicly. History museums exist first to keep and develop, for more than one life-time, material and aural records of social experience and secondly to explore key themes and issues from this to a present day audience. Essentially, museums have long term purposes and short term ends. If this is accepted, and clearly it is by a significant proportion of curators, then history museums have vital functions to perform. To keep a grip on histories rather than stories, a museum has to be led forward by social and intellectual convictions, rather than primarily economic ones. To put it another way, ultimately it needs to be mission- rather than market-led. As Peter Ames (1988) has pointed out, the trick is getting the mix right. A museum that is primarily market led, to my mind, ends up by not being a museum.

The comparison with museum developments in America is useful here. Michael Wallace in an article called the 'Politics of public history' considers the powerful role American museums play in re-enforcing myths about the past (1987). In so doing he nevertheless envisages the museum as an institution superbly situated to inform people of the continuities between past and present. But he draws attention to the ways in which public histories in American museums are produced for a 'market', as a commodity, which people don't have to buy if they don't want to. He writes:

> Consumers have their own conventions and assumptions and tend not to gravitate to presentations that don't re-enforce these. For producers who aim to *change* their audiences'

A fully integrated approach to exhibition is taken at the Museum of the Moving Image in London.

minds on some matter, the prior necessity of attracting them as customers can act as a drag on innovation. But more often than not, I suspect, audience conservatism is simply taken for granted. The cry that something 'won't sell' is often used as an excuse by those who want a program killed on other grounds. [But] conventional wisdoms are fluid things; audiences change with the times, and when challenged, often respond favorably. Witness the triumph of *Roots* in a culture once seemingly mired in the pieties of *Gone With the Wind* (Wallace 1987:43).

I join with the notion that museums in an effort to locate a commercial position have radically underestimated the public's interest in and ability to cope with challenging and alternative views of the past and present. Many museums have avoided issues and topics well within their remit. The tried and tested safe routes have been preferred. Indeed preconceptions about the public's level of competence have been allowed to act as a 'drag on innovation'. However, indisputably the potential is there: museums can create very direct records that touch to the quick the essence of human experience. The work in Glasgow of the People's Palace and of late, Springburn Museum provides us with ample evidence of this.

Exhibitions as Historiography
Museums make their histories primarily through the medium of exhibition, supplemented and extended through education programmes and publications. We are poorly served in this regard in that, unlike other forms of history text, exhibitions do not receive peer group or public criticism of their messages. Curators therefore largely extend their skills on comparison of form (lighting, type of graphics used. . . .) rather than content (material included, excluded, meaning ascribed . . .). This point has been made many times over the years and is as valid now as it has ever been. The involvement of academics, teachers and local historians in round table discussions about the content of an exhibition is something to be encouraged.

But is it appropriate to consider exhibition as a form of historiography, which should be open to peer group criticism? I believe so, even though the word 'history' referring to all museums that address some aspect of the recent human past, from costume museums, through social history museums to transport galleries, is an inadequate catch-all term. However, for as long as history museums lay claim to the past, they ought to be open to criticism from an historiographic viewpoint.

There are three principal traditions in the writing of history: narrative, descriptive and analytical. The *narrative* tradition comes closest to story-telling. It is the historian's most basic way of relating a sequence of events. Chronological patterns and strict areas of theme are maintained. The reader is led through time, with little opportunity or encouragement to consider causation, effects or complex issues of context. Narrative at its best is a form of explanation of events and characters. *Descriptive* writing concentrates on presenting a visual image or impression of a person, idea or event. It is generally composed of statements of fact and interpretation, dealing with a restricted moment in time. *Analytical* history is the most common form and the most difficult to write. It seeks to lay bare the true nature of an event or episode, not just through an appreciation of the causes and results. The discovery of the way people thought, felt, and were motivated is central to this form of history writing. In style, analytical writing may involve both narrative and description, but is distinctive for its questioning of all sources and received truths.

Analysing exhibitions against these three traditions presents difficulties; they just do not relate that easily. However, it is possible to suggest exhibition forms that roughly fit each category. The Royal Naval Museum in Portsmouth takes the visitor through a narrative of the navy's history. The narrative, given in panels of graphics and illustrations, is punctuated with objects. Collectively these lead the visitor through an essentially progressive history of the British Navy. Most museums that attempt to 're-create' a period or a process are dealing in the main in a descriptive style of history-making. The open-air museums with their reconstructed houses, furnished and fitted to pin-point one moment in time are essentially descriptive. Their concern is to describe how things were, leaving the visitor to draw conclusions about how things have changed. *Why* things have changed enters the realms of analysis and this is often absent.

The analytical is far harder to identify in museum exhibitions, but it can be found. The current exhibition at Nordiska Museet in Stockholm called *Modell Sverige* attempts to explain how and why Sweden has changed over the last 130 years from being a largely self-sufficient peasant society into one of the western world's most advanced social democratic states. Through the use of comparisons and carefully selected symbols, the exhibition looks at changes in the nature of work, social and domestic environments, power and energy, and the roles of women. Through the use of film, it also considers wider issues, such as Sweden on the world's stage. This willingness to pose questions was also evident in the same museum's exhibition which explored the nature of long distance travel. This was staged in 1982. Instead of holding up a sequence of gleaming vehicles in chronological order for the public's admiration, as grown-up dinky toys, the museum presented an exhibition that considered not only how people travelled long distances but who such people were. The underlying point was that from the earliest coaches to modern jet plane, long distant travel has been the prerogative of the more wealthy. To present such thought-provoking exhibitions, in forms which excite the imagination and promote natural curiosity, and to do so in ways that make the reading of labels not essential to the communication of the exhibition's argument, demonstrates something of a museum's capacity to analyse, as well as describe and narrate.

History in museums tends to be offered in a descriptive form because the principle medium, objects, appear to offer few alternatives. How can cultural and social change be discussed through material which is so fixed in its form? How can life, which is essentially active and changing, be explained by things which are essentially lifeless and therefore constant? The answer to this lies in the ways we understand objects as evidence, the ways in which meanings ascribed to them change, and the museum's ability to juxtapose images and objects.

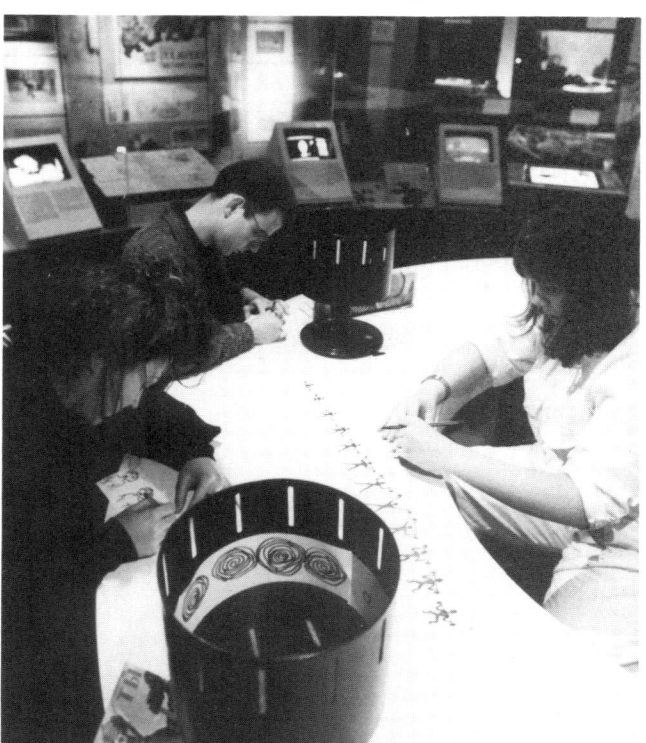

The formal displays in the animation gallery are supported by demonstration and participation.

This is far more than an issue of exhibition techniques. It relates to all the fundamental processes of fieldwork, acquisition, documentation and collections care. The museum's message directly corresponds to the degree to which history is grasped by curators.

Per-Uno Ågren and Göran Carlsson in their excellent book *Utställningsspråk* (1982) provide us with a means of categorizing forms of exhibition. These can be understood on one level as springing from traditions of exhibition-making, but can also be viewed as indicating the depth of understanding about the past a museum brings to the public through its exhibitions. Ågren and Carlsson have five categories of what they call 'exhibition language'.

The first is *mass* where a complete collection, or an extremely broad selection of objects are shown together, usually un-labelled. Often associated with local, possibly amateur-run museums, this form of exhibition is in fact sometimes encountered in the most polished of museums. In this form, objects tumble over each other in a chaos through which visitors must pick and choose their own paths, making assumptions and guesses as they go. Used as a visual break, with objects that have established meaning, this can sometimes be an interesting way of looking at things. But more often than not, the mass approach is disorganized jumble. It is the farthest that a museum can move away from explaining the past.

The second form identified by Ågren and Carlsson is a *label* exhibition. This is where objects are ordered in seried ranks with basic labels identifying the name, donor, provenance and classification number of each. This is a classical approach to exhibition. As long ago as 1895, museum curators were being instructed that 'an efficient educational Museum may be described as a collection of instructive labels, each illustrated by a well chosen specimen' (Goode Brown 1895: 108). Avoiding anything that might approach context or comment, such exhibitions provide little more than a visual catalogue. Where nothing more than a type series is required, the label exhibition can suffice.

The exhibition form takes a massive leap forward with the *thematic,* which deals with strictly defined topics. This is a very familiar form of exhibition in Britain. It applies where material is brought together under broad headings, sometimes derived from the museum's classification system. Thus one finds exhibitions headed 'domestic life', 'law and order', 'dairying', 'local trades' or 'toys'. With limited extension of the selected theme through the use of photographs and some general, explanatory labels, such exhibitions tend not to move beyond the technical or descriptive.

The fourth form identified by Ågren and Carlsson is the *narrative.* This is where the exhibition form has been developed to communicate a point of view or narrate an experience. Usually employing fieldwork, the results of active collecting and the actual words of local people, the narrative form relies on the use of very diverse media. At a further and more advanced level, this evolves into the final category, *total* or comprehensive exhibition. This form is distinguished by the use of many different exhibition styles and techniques to allow active exploration of the museum's subject. Objects, illustrations, photographs, texts, light, colour, movement, texture, smell, noise, video, re-constructions, models are joined together in ways that allow many different access points to the exhibition's theme. Moreover, the element of choice is built in so that people can elect to learn more and can select what they are particularly interested in. Communication is extended and maximised through the use of drama and educational programmes within the exhibition area, and through the use of publications, both learned and popular.

This total approach is increasingly found in museums. The most recent and perhaps well-developed example in Britain is at the Museum of the Moving Image (MOMI) in London. Although well aware of the ease with which affective learning can take place, dealing as it does with the media which is the core of twentieth century life, at no point does MOMI appear to lose an opportunity for cognitive learning. It leads the visitor from the familiar to the unfamiliar, from established knowledge to new understanding. And it does this by providing a 'total' approach, which has pace, choice and opportunity. The 'total' approach is not confined to well-funded or new museums. It can be seen used in many science museums and provincial museums, such as Västerbottens Museum, in Northern Sweden.

Such a complex form of exhibition is only possible and indeed viable where there is a considerable depth of understanding and a solid range of collections and documentation on which to draw. In the case of Västerbottens Museum, the re-display of the museum, completed in 1982, museum staff were able to call on the experience of much fieldwork, in particular an excellent film archive and collections built up painstakingly over many years. The exhibitions there, as with other examples of the total approach, are derived from professional, long term curatorship. It is this that gives them their social credibility and intellectual worth. Add to this an infectious regard for people (past and present), the willingness to communicate to visitors of all ages and sizes, and the originality of mind that can break away from established traditions of what a museum exhibition should look like, and we start seeing exhibitions of the calibre of those at MOMI and Västerbottens museum.

Considering the five forms of exhibition language suggested by Ågren and Carlsson, it can be suggested that the more adventurous and challenging an exhibition form becomes, the greater the need to have a grasp of the complexities of history and the range of evidence being offered. Without this, the complexities of the 'total' approach collapse. Instead of offering a choice of tantalizing routes into an interesting subject, the material falls about in a 'mass'. The circle turns and the museum is back at the most rudimentary and confusing of exhibition forms.

Opportunities and Future Directions
There are many areas of presenting histories in museums that warrant our attention. Three can be dealt with here: labels; the involvement of people in the presentation of what is after all their histories; and the new and far more critical audiences museums will be attracting in the years ahead.

With regard to labelling, curators have been concerned with length of text and its readability. Both of these areas have established literature, very well known to museum studies students past and present (for example Hartley, 1978, and Serrel, 1983). What we now need to look at very carefully is what is actually being said. A study of labelling as a specific area of museum historiography is long overdue, although some work in this area is currently underway.

The whole process of label writing is perhaps one of the most under-rated elements of professional practice. It produces a very specific form of 'literature'. The writing of texts for exhibition, not only requires getting the facts straight, but also selecting the most relevant pieces of information, incorporating them in a style that excites the imagination and promotes curiosity, while at the same time using words that are easy to consume by people who are on their feet and on the move.

It is interesting that in Sweden the state exhibition service has employed an author, Margareta Ekarv, to write labels and exhibition texts from information supplied by curators. She has worked on a number of successful projects including the Postmuseum in Stockholm. One of her points of reference is her experience writing books for adults learning to read. Such books contain language that is clear and texts that are interesting, but which do not condescend to the reader. In contrast, Ekarv sees much curatorial language used in labels as being 'laced with academic grooming, abstract and long-winded'. Ekarv argues that museum text should be written so that it can be spoken. Its content should be such that it makes people think and inter-act with what they see. She also suggests that labels could be written drawing on a variety of literary forms including poetry.

To my mind, an under-utilized form of museum label is one that draws directly on the words of the very people who used the objects on display or experienced something of the subject being discussed. Where this approach has been employed, it gives the exhibition a directness and impact which is unparalleled. In these instances the museum ceases to be overtly interventionist in the view it offers of the past and goes someway to hand back the narration and explanation of the past to the true experts, the people who lived it.

The new exhibitions at the People's Story in Edinburgh I believe will profoundly benefit from direct in-put from local people and will provide a model which I hope will influence other museums (Beevers 1988). The sharpness of work developing through Age Exchange Theatre in London is also directly attributable to this willingness to share and not appropriate history. In the case of Age Exchange, it is interesting that their oral history programmes, reminiscence therapy, performance, publications and exhibitions are now leading them to create a museum. Museums are moving the opposite way, from collections through fieldwork and exhibitions to performance. If we all meet in the same place then museum provision in Britain will be very rich indeed.

Recent educational changes will have a significant influence on the histories museums produce. Changes to the GCSE history syllabuses have resulted in as much weight being given to evidence as to narrative content. As a result, in time, visiting children (who grow swiftly into adults, tax-payers, and sometimes museum trustees) will be viewing exhibitions from very different standpoints. Through such educational changes, a greater proportion of museum visitors will have minds trained to question what they see, look for the omissions and detect the biases in history presentation. They should be capable of asking why and how museum exhibitions are put together and able to judge the 'history' a museum thinks it is offering. Exhibitions grandly entitled 'Victorian Things', or 'Transport Through the Ages' may receive a response hitherto not experienced by museum from their visitors: healthy criticism of content.

These matters are important in improving professional standards in museums, something which has an increasing sense of urgency within what has been heralded as a commercial market place. Museum staff are being exhorted to improve museum images and the quality of the 'experiences' they provide. Such exhortations often fall on those who have committed a lifetime to improving services and expanding museum audiences to all sectors and not just those mobile enough and affluent enough to have access to a past packaged as being theirs. It is small wonder that there is anguish amongst the ranks of curators when large sums of public money are given to projects within the commercial heritage industry, which must of their very nature be ephemeral and therefore not likely to last more than fifteen or twenty years, if that.

The Scottish Museums Council is to be applauded for stating unambiguously in *A Framework for Museums in Scotland* that public funds should not be invested in new museums, unless certain safeguards prevail. In this instance it is unfortunate that the word 'museum' can not extend to some forms of related enterprises. This is not just a matter of professional self-defence. Museums are by anybody's calculation the best long term investment for public and private funds, if visitor figures and studies such as that undertaken by the Policy Studies Institute, *The Economic Importance of the Arts in Britain* (1988), are taken into account. Indeed this wide ranging and important survey re-iterates the need to develop existing initiatives. Consolidation and expansion of existing museum resources seems to me to be a matter of extreme common sense. Regrettably, however, the attraction of the new may always be more tantalising and seductive than developing the old.

We need to cast our thoughts to the future and question how long some of the current trends can last. Although we need to be very wary of taking evidence from outside Britain and using it as a predictor for trends here, a number of trends in America are worth noting. I offer the next two pieces of information as food for thought, no more.

Firstly in the United States, many cities have developed what has been described as 'lures of cultural-historical interest' and in this cause museums have been opened, the heritage industry explored, and convention centres built. But the social and economic realities such initiatives are aimed at smoothing or masking over still prevail. Questions are now being asked about 'how many museums, cultural centres, convention and exhibition halls, hotels, marinas and shopping malls can a place take?'

Narrative exhibitions, such as this one on reindeer husbandry, interpret through linking together objects, photographs, text and testimony.

Evidence from the United States suggests general over-investment and over-production in all these spheres. A major disaster may be in the offing (Harvey 1988).

A contributing factor in such a crash may be the second piece of information worthy of your attention: in the United States there have been significant changes in leisure patterns. A national survey conducted by the National Research Center of the Arts, *Americans and the Arts V,* has revealed a 37% decrease in leisure hours since 1973. This has resulted in increased competition in the leisure industry. Museum audiences being drawn from the more affluent sector of society are less affected by such trends, but nevertheless museums now have to work consciously to maintain their current audiences and harder still to extend into new areas. I would suggest that such trends should be taken as a scenario worth contemplating.

Conclusions
The potential both of history in museums and history museums in society, in general terms has been little grasped. But the evidence we have of it comes from the work and convictions of the most professional generation of history curators the museum world has seen. This leads to a number of conclusions.

Firstly, a museum should not only inform people and create opportunities for learning, it should also move them too. Anger, pride, laughter and tears are evidence of our affective learning from and about the past. They increase our capacity for congnitive learning, for getting to the facts of a matter. Histories without feelings or true understanding are hollow stories. Museums that convey them are shell and no substance.

Secondly, a museum should be a context for many different personal activities. People reach histories through asking, reading, writing, watching, listening, telling, presenting and performing. The museum can bring all of these together in one place and provide a context in which images are built and opinions formed. A successful museum is one that is a forum for debate, a place for discovery, an environment for questions.

Thirdly, the museum is a legitimizing institution. It therefore finds itself with considerable power. Because of this, we should be concerned about the differences between histories and heritage, learning and packaging, interpretation and interference. On the one hand the images created by museums can buttress social identity, and consolidate social positions and class interests. On the other hand they can enable the opening of new ideas and the articulation of long silent questions. They can even provide the basis for an agenda for change.

The future for history in museums will depend upon many factors. Perhaps most important of these is what we believe a museum to be and the forms it should take. It has to be said that many museums cling to narrow traditions and out-dated dogmas, the wreckage of vessels that began to disintegrate some twenty years ago. Perhaps the concern has been too much about what a museum *should look like.* This has given way to the ubiquitous displays of Victorian kitchens, sitting rooms and craftsman's workshops. In its stead, convictions about what a museum *should be* can lead to recording, collecting and interpretative functions that continually break new ground and refuse to be confined by established conventions.

In the final analysis, it may prove that the museums with well considered social and intellectual purposes, some solid sense of their current and future roles, will be able not just to survive but thrive in the years ahead. In such places histories will be found. Pots of myths and packages of stories will be absent, because people of the present and the past deserve better.

Bibliography

Ames, P. (1988) 'A challenge to modern museum management; reconciling mission and market', *Museum Studies Journal,* Spring-Summer. San Francisco.

Beevers, L. et al (1988) Memories and Things. *Linking Museums and Libraries with Older People.* Edinburgh.

Boyle, N. (1988) 'Thatchers' dead souls', *New Statesman and Society,* 14 October, London.

Carlsson, G. and Ågren, P-U. (1982) Utställningsspråk, Stockholm.

Goode, G. B., 1895. 'The principles of Museum Administration', Museums Association. Report of the Proceedings at the Sixth Annual General Meeting: 69-148. London.

Hartley, J. (1978) *Designing Instructional Text.* London.

Harvey, D. (1988) 'Voodoo cities', *New Statesman and Society,* 30 September. London.

Myerscough, J. et al (1988) *The Economic Importance of the Arts in Britain.* London.

Scottish Museums Council (1988) *A Framework for Museums in Scotland.* Edinburgh.

Serrel, B. (1983) *Making exhibit labels: A Step by Step Guide.* Nashville.

Wallace, M. (1987) 'The politics of public history' in J Blatti (ed) *Past meets Present. Essays about Historic Interpretation and Public Audiences.* Washington.

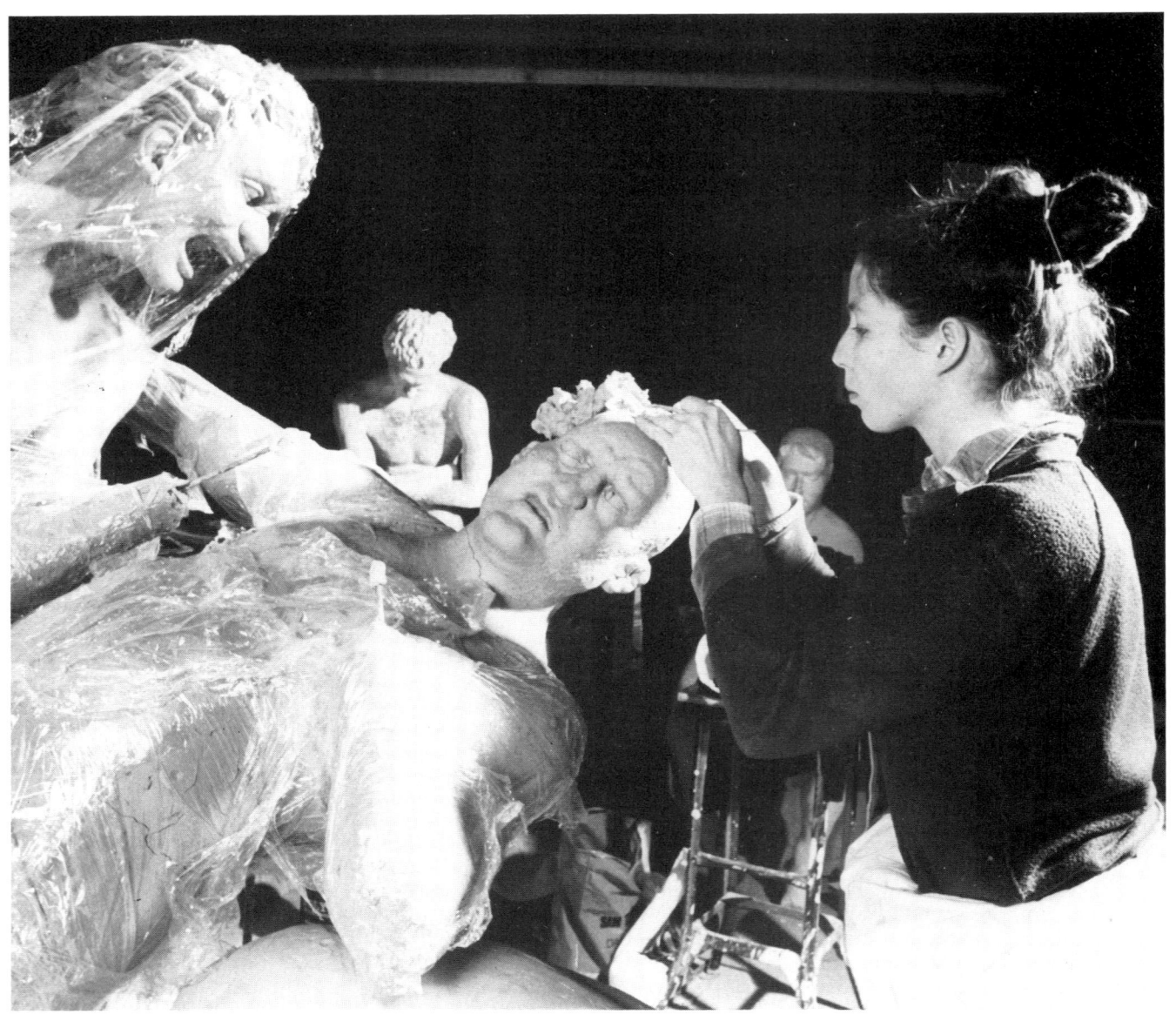
Making models for the Oxford Story in Heritage Projects Workshops.

PEOPLING THE PAST
– THE FUTURE OF HERITAGE PRESENTATION

Anthony Gaynor

Anthony Gaynor OBE, former Managing Director of Cultural Resource Management Ltd and Heritage Projects Ltd. He created the successful Jorvik Viking Centre at York and other projects including the Oxford Story and the Pilgrims' Way Canterbury have followed. The Edinburgh Story is in preparation.

I would like to begin this paper by analysing what I think are the activities undertaken within the museum profession, a very incautious thing of me to try, but I believe it is nonetheless relevant as a starting point for the arguments presented below.

I would argue that one of the activities which museums undertake most successfully is *conservation*. Now I know this breaks down into many areas, but to a non-specialist like me *'conservation'* is a useful overall umbrella term which covers large buildings, small buildings, artefacts of various natures and types, and so on.

The next activity I would suggest is *research*, and this again is an umbrella term which encompasses making collections and information available to research students outside museums, as well as carrying out research within museums using their own collections and information.

There is a third aspect which is *display*. It is on this area that I really want to concentrate because to put it bluntly, I think that there is a blurring of these three primary activities by the museum profession. Certainly, there has been in the past, but I think that progress is now being made in the separation of these various functions. Nonetheless they are not totally separate, and the display function is one which the non-specialist public understands best. It is the display function which provides the interface with the non-specialist, and frankly, this is the area where I feel that I have the greatest expertise.

Changing Times

There is an increasing public interest in the past. We all know that. Whether this is a substitute for formal religion; whether this is a recognition of the fact that people have more leisure time; whether it's because people are looking for 'roots' or heritage, or whatever it is, there is an increasing interest in the past, and an increasing recognition of its relevance to the future. It is quite frightening, certainly in a military context, how the mistakes of the past tend to be repeated in the present and unless we are very careful will be repeated in the future. This applies to all sorts of disciplines and aspects of life and therefore the past is relevant to the future. It is also a fact that public sector funding for the various activities relating to the museum profession is not nearly as generous as everybody would like. At the same time there is an ever increasing requirement for spending on all sorts of very worthy activities. To take just one, with our ageing population and with the increased sophistication of medicine in general, people are living longer, and therefore the Health Service in all its various disciplines and factions is expected to be a bottomless bucket. No matter how much money is poured into it, there would still be a reasonable argument to be made for *more* money to be spent on it. This is the climate in which we are competing for resources and frankly, I can't see that ever being different.

Now my contention is that it makes commercial sense actually to emphasise that aspect of your profession which is the most readily visible by the public, and enjoys the highest public sympathy, and that for museums, is *display*. That is not to undermine in any sense the other two activities and the sub-divisions of those two activities because they are clearly highly relevant, very necessary, but they are nonetheless very specialised. I have been associated with the world of archaeology for ten or eleven years now, and I know how specialised it can be. I have every reason to believe that other disciplines within the museum profession are equally specialised and require an equal amount of loving care and attention. So I take my argument one step further and say if your resources are scarce – a situation not going to be remedied in the foreseeable future by Central Government funding – and if you have a resource (your collections), and in addition you have a public demand to look at those collections, then you must make the most of them. Making the most of what you've got is not a bad principle in life anyway. I can give you a concrete example of how it has worked using my company, Heritage Projects Ltd, over the last six or seven years.

Now these are the development criteria we use at Heritage Projects:

>Academic Accuracy
>Public Acceptability
>Commercial Viability

I would like to discuss each one in turn:
Academic accuracy. This is the absolute cornerstone of our operation. In the various displays that we've mounted – and I'll discuss them briefly later – the academic content and the interpretation of the message can of course be criticised, but it can be criticised at an academic level. For example, take our development at Oxford – the Oxford Story. We have had a great deal of correspondence about the accuracy or otherwise of certain of the gable-ended buildings that we have put in one of the sets there. Now I think that is healthy, because at least by putting up what is a best guess of what is or what would have been a 13th century gable-ended building in Oxford, we are open to intelligent and sensible criticism. No-one is saying that it is total and utter falsehood, but they are able to say 'in my opinion it would be much more sensible if . . .' And so, simply by producing display, we are provoking discussion at an academic level and that in itself cannot be a bad thing.

Secondly, *Public Acceptability* – this really ensures that we do not get into highly controversial areas. Would you believe I was seriously approached by a charity who wanted me to build a Museum of Slavery? Well, frankly I had to decline that one, and I do not think I would ever develop a Tobacco Museum. There is a certain underlying commerciality in the way which I approach this in that on the one hand, I do not want to provoke antagonism and on the other hand, I want to spread the appeal as widely as possible because our third criterion is also essential: *Commercial Viability*. We are a commercial company. Let's not get away from that.

The story started with archaeology at York and the fact that there was a charity, a provincial charity, which was largely centrally Government funded and which had chronic cash problems. What was its asset? Well, when I joined them, the answer was 'A bloody big hole in the middle of York' and precious little else. And so, the first thing we did was to make that asset scarce by putting a fence round it and charging people to go in.

About five years later, having established that there was a public demand to learn about Vikings, the York Archaeological Trust built the Viking Centre which opened in 1984. Now it is of interest here that it is owned by the charity, not by me: I built it; I run it in every aspect; but I don't own it. I wish I did, but I don't! That was one of my mistakes in life!

The Jorvik Viking Centre is owned by a charity, it is run as a commercial activity, it is academically correct. The Director of the British Museum, Sir David Wilson, who is himself a specialist on Vikings and the Saxon period, said it was 'smashing', which made a jolly good press release. I think that he was unhappy about certain aspects of it, but that is inevitable. But, and here is the big 'but', this development which cost £2.6 million now nets just about £1 million a year for that charity. It is very easy to say, 'Well it's just too easy. Just build the thing and you know there are lots of tourists in York and it's bound to succeed.' However, five or six years ago when I was trying to fund an underground museum of archaeology owned by a charity with no track record and no security, it was hard going — but we did it. So all I'm saying is that it can and has been done. Despair not. Even if

The Time Tunnel at the Joruik Viking Centre, York.

you are wrapped round by local government provisions and all sorts of charitable trust deeds, there is a way if you have a small and determined team to fight your way through the red tape and the local opposition and build yourself a solution that will solve your financial problems, without prejudicing your academic stance.

We have opened *The Pilgrim Way* in Canterbury, which is working very well now. We have converted a church to tell the story of the murder of Thomas à Beckett and Chaucer's Canterbury Tales. When it opened in March 1988, it got off to a slow start. We solved the technical problems, and now it is going very well indeed. We are very happy with that one.

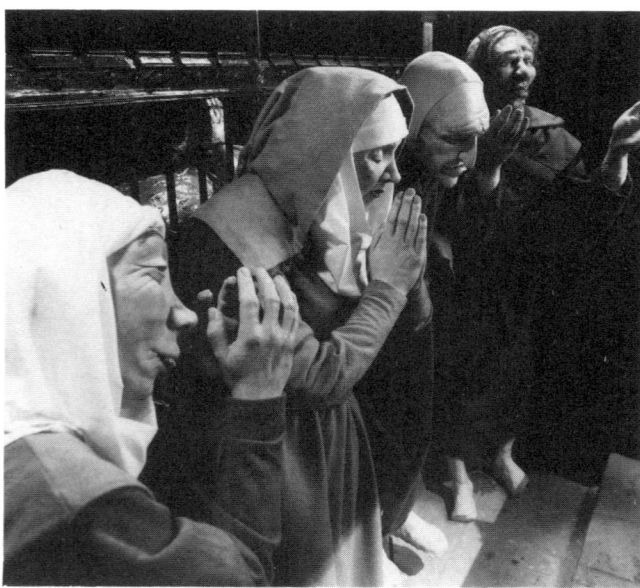

Pilgrims at the Shrine, Pilgrims Way, Canterbury.

At Oxford, the *Oxford Story* is a joint development with Oxford University, telling the achievements of some of the undergraduates and some of the activities that go on at Oxford. We had a great disappointment there with the mechanical ride system which didn't work. We've got an off-site rig now working. The financial implications of installing that ride are being addressed. I personally am not very happy with quite a bit of it. It lacks magic and I think that that magic would have been there had we got the ride working correctly. But, we are in the risk business. We are a commercial company. We will sort it out.

Lastly, a word about the *Edinburgh Story* in the Tollbooth, that very large kirk at the top end of the Royal Mile in Edinburgh. The scheme has caused us great problems — some of our own making, most of them not, and when one looks back over the history of it, the crucial thing that has presented us with the greatest problem is the delay in the approval of all the funding packages, a delay of five months during which time we were not able to get on site for legal reasons. Had we started on site, we would have rendered void certain of the grants and have been deemed to have taken on the lease of the building before the funding had been totally approved. But I was not prepared to take on a fully repairing and insuring lease on a great church like that until I knew I had the funding package. I had every assurance that the funding would come and that the various agencies and the offices and authorities would stand by what they said, and indeed they did.

During that five-month period over the winter, the rot which we knew was in the church became absolutely rampant and therefore we have got problems which we are eradicating at the moment with regard to the roof and various other parts of the church. This has caused a large over-run on budget, which is straining the financial viability. I'm not prepared to go into further detail at this stage: we are discussing with our fellow agencies whether the funding of the over-run is wholly to us. The nature of the display in the building is unchanged. Our commitment to it as I said earlier on is £2.5 million with which these days you can still do a great deal. And so, that's where we are with the Tollbooth.

Now, what about the future? I believe that in this business the future is every bit as relevant as the past, and I think I should — warn is too strong a word — draw your attention to the fact that museums are going to get substantial competition from the newly built academic resource-type building. There are a lot of out-of-town retail developments; there are an awful lot of in-town retail developments; and the market has caught on to the fact that education is a commercial adjunct to lots of other leisure activities. So there is a market for non-specialist *'museums'* such as I build, centres which have academic validity. There is going to be increasing competition for museums. Museums should be aware that there are some very large developments indeed about to be announced which will inject competition into the fairly tranquil waters in which they now exist.

The interior of the Tollbooth Kirk, Edinburgh, undergoing changes.

Our newest scheme, which we have submitted for planning purposes, is for a Space development. Basically it is about £15 million worth of space, not in Scotland, but in England. It satisfies the three criteria which I identified earlier on: academic accuracy, public acceptability, and financial viability.

It will be built in the middle of one of the biggest out-of-town shopping centres in Britain, probably one of the biggest in Europe. At first it may appear ridiculous — Disney gone mad. Well, first, I like Disney anyway, and secondly, this development is going to tell the story of the history of space, space travel, the myths and mythology, Dan Dare, 'Journey into Space', 'Hitchhikers Guide to the Galaxy' — and a lot more. It will also describe Russian and American and European space activities and will include astronomy. It will be fun, it will be big, it will be reasonably expensive, but it will be there. So this is the kind of development coming up on the outside

lane. I imagine that many readers will have been to La Villette, the French science museum in the northern suburbs of Paris on the old slaughterhouse site. Well, our plans combine that approach with a bit of Disney. So the plans for this type of development are on a large scale and so is the money coming from the private sector to fund them.

To my mind then, there is no reason why education and entertainment of the public in academically valid topics should be regarded as the exclusive preserve of the academic profession — that exclusivity has gone. The input to the design comes from the academic professions but their right to display that has gone. It has been taken from them. The museum professionals have a tremendous advantage, however, in that they are the custodians of the artefacts which make such displays valid.

So I return to my original point: there are difficulties for museums with their collections — under-funding, leaking roofs, and archives and so on — I know the problems. But, don't call them problems, call them challenges. Make them positive because new developments are coming up on the outside track. Today's public are increasingly demanding — stereo sound, full colour, interactive computers — are all completely normal means of communication to the young. They are now the standard means of communication for a quarter of the public, and increasingly large parts of the museum-going public. So if museums are going to stay in the running they are going to have to go with this new tide. We are all in a highly competitive market. I have got my competitors at my end of the industry; museums have their competitors elsewhere. We've got to survive and I think that museums can only survive if they take the display element of their activities and major on it, to generate the income to subsidise their other very valid but less publicly appealing activities.

Leith Hall – dining room.

THE NATIONAL TRUST FOR SCOTLAND — PRESENTING SCOTLAND'S HISTORIC HOUSES

David Learmont

David Learmont has been Curator at the National Trust for Scotland since 1970, responsible for the interiors and contents of the Trust's properties. He is particularly associated with Culzean, the Georgian House, Gladstone's Land, Fyvie Castle and now House of Dun. He is a founder member of the Furniture History Society and a Fellow of the Society of Antiquaries.

The National Trust for Scotland was founded in 1931 to promote the preservation of Scotland's heritage of fine buildings, beautiful landscape and historic places, and to encourage public enjoyment of them. Properties came into the care of the National Trust for Scotland in different ways and for a variety of reasons. In the case of Leith Hall in Aberdeenshire, it was a family tragedy. The property came to the Trust in 1945 following the death of the last laird at a very early age at the beginning of the Second World War. The Bachelor's Club at Tarbolton, by contrast, belonged to a local amenity society and passed to the Trust before the war when the officers died. In the case of Fyvie Castle it was quite simply 'Trust or bust'.

When a property is acquired by the Trust and is to be opened to the public there is usually much work to be done on it first. Decisions on how it should be rehabilitated or restored or recreated are made in each individual case at the end of a lengthy process of analysis and discussion of every detail. In the case studies given here we show how we responded to very different challenges, always striving to 'get it right', from the fenestration to the fireplaces and the furnishings.

Leith Hall

We look first at Leith Hall, which was built in the 1650s as a tower house, to which two wings were added in the 18th century and further additions were made in the 19th century, so that the three-storied house has a central courtyard. Leith Hall was in the same family, the Leiths and Leith-Hays, for 300 years, during which time a great quantity of objects, paintings and furniture was collected. The house had been divided and let in three parts for many years and in 1984 we decided to show more of it to the public with its contents to demonstrate the family's fortunes.

Fortunately there was not a great deal of structural work to be done: the house retained its original chimneypieces — good provincial ones with their original grates supplied by the Carron Company.

Many of the pictures had been stored away above the stables but they were recovered and restored. The needlework was in good condition. I think the dining room now best conveys to the visitor the family atmosphere we wanted to achieve. It is furnished from the family collections and hung with a good selection of family portraits. There is a superb fireplace of steel inlaid with brass.

The Bachelors' Club

The Bachelors' Club at Tarbolton, near Ayr, contrasts sharply with Leith Hall demonstrating the variety of properties in the care of the National Trust for Scotland. It is one of the very few thatched houses left in Scotland. It takes its name from the weekly debating society which Robert Burns helped to set up in 1780. It was in this house that Burns was admitted to the local Freemasons' Lodge in 1781. The upstairs room contains items associated with Burns, and the dimly-lit downstairs room is furnished as a kitchen of the period, complete with stone floor and cloutie (rag) rugs, box bed, deal table and chairs, spinning wheel, meal kist, open fire with bellows, kettle on the hob and pots hanging from a swee.

Bachelors' Club, Tarbolton.

The house passed to the Trust from a local society in the 1930s and was in a poor state. We found reed thatchers from Norfolk to repair the roof and furnished the interior with items given to us by members, basing our presentation on Wilkie engravings.

Gladstone's Land

Gladstone's Land on the Royal Mile was saved before the war by a public-spirited individual and presented to the Trust. It is an excellent example of an Edinburgh 'land' or tenement, called after Thomas Gledstanes who bought the property in 1617. Following the success of the Georgian House, we decided in 1980 to furnish it as an Edinburgh merchant's house, dating back to the end of the 17th century, with a period shop on the ground floor. We began with the exterior, recreating the arcaded entrance to the shop at street level and restoring the fenestration. The lower half of the windows are now shuttered with oak and the upper part glazed with small panes of glass.

Creating a shop on the ground floor was a challenge because there were very few good illustrations of 17th century shop interiors for guidance, and most of them were examples from the Low Countries. We created a dimly-lit booth stocked with rough woollen cloth for sale. Lengths of cloth were woven, only a yard of each, which were wrapped around cardboard dummies to stock the shelves. The nice old scissors we found have had to be rivetted to the table for security.

A narrow, winding, stone staircase gives access to the living rooms on the first floor. There is a dimly-lit, small sitting room and a kitchen where a flagstone floor was laid and a wall-bed installed, based on one which survives at Culross. We managed to find a suitably worn-looking grate and a general collection of furniture and utensils, mostly Scottish, in the same tradition. The large principal room of the house is also on this floor at the front. As was customary, it served both as a living room and bedroom. The ceiling had been restored in the 1930s using a wax treatment that had become badly discoloured. This had to be removed and the original was restored by the Stenhouse Conservation Centre. This experience reinforced for us the importance of only carrying out reversible procedures in conservation — which is standard modern practice. On the wall above the fireplace we had painted a frieze of simple arches to give an indication of how the original painted decoration might have appeared. The room was furnished with a four-post bed of the Aberdeen school and early oak pieces, and the walls hung with linen below the painted decoration.

Behind these rooms there was one other room, the Green Room, which was early 18th century, c. 1720-1740. We decided to use it to show the transition between the life-style of the Old Town and the New Town as exemplified in the Georgian House, Charlotte Square. The room was all stripped out and the original dark green colour scheme was restored. We replaced a cupboard with its utility door with a display cupboard made in our own workshops. There is a simple bolection fireplace and early Georgian furniture. We have hung a collection of Dutch paintings which is probably too important to be on display in this room, but we were given them by a very generous benefactor who is able to see them there.

Drum Castle

Drum Castle in Aberdeenshire came to us in 1976. It is a house of great charm consisting of three parts in three distinct styles of architecture that reflect the changing fortunes of one family, the Irvines, who owned the castle for 650 years. The three granite buildings blend together so well it is hard to believe that they consist of a massive tower dating from the 13th century; the south front, a stately mansion dating from 1619; and the north range which was added in 1875.

The rooms were very unprepossessing, but we managed to make the house live again by getting the 'bones' of the rooms right, installing the hob grates and using as much furniture as possible which was already in the house. This was only augmented by suitable surplus items from other properties. Two Victorian bedrooms were created out of virtually nothing. Fortunately we had some very good bequests at that time. As always we aimed to get the correct historical colour scheme reinstated, without being too academic.

We had a photograph of the kitchen as it appeared in about 1890, complete with hot cross-buns on the table. After the war it had been re-designed, so we took on a functional kitchen with a linoleum floor, a discreet boiler in the corner and a nice red sink. It has now been restored as nearly as possible to its late 19th century appearance — the only omissions are the hot-cross buns!

Fyvie Castle

When the contents of Fyvie, that great castle in Aberdeenshire, were about to be dispersed, a number of public bodies intervened at short notice, and finally thanks to the generous support of the National Heritage Memorial Fund, the property and its contents were conveyed to the Trust.

Much of the castle was remodelled at the end of the 19th century in a very grand, opulent manner. It was decided to maintain this character in all its eccentricities by recapturing and reintroducing the colour schemes and furniture arrangements of the period. The house had been redecorated before the war in the fashion of those days and the wall coverings had to be replaced in favour of something more appropriate. The interior now appears much as it might have done at the beginning of the century, with much of its own character and that of the people who lived there being retained.

The billiard room was in a neglected state, but we managed to reproduce the original colour scheme. The curtains, pelmets, lampshades and loose covers, however, had to be replaced.

The dining room in the Gordon Tower dating from 1790 had been refurnished in the 1890s and we have recaptured this later decoration using a red damask wallpaper similar to that used originally. It makes a splendid background for the collection of portraits.

The Morning Room, which had been the drawing room in the 18th century and the High Hall in the 17th century, is shown as an informal family sitting room as it was when the Forbes-Leiths lived in the castle. The decorative plaster ceiling was much discoloured and had to be repainted. Unfortunately eggshell paint was used to begin with which emphasised the irregularities in the surface and so it had to be redone in flat oil paint. The room is dominated by a large Flemish tapestry.

Fyvie has a superb collection of pictures. The Raeburns – the best collection outside the National Galleries of Scotland – are shown together in the Back Morning Room where they make a magnificent display. Probably the most ravishing is that of Mrs Gregory – by family tradition there were always white flowers in a vase below it – a tradition which we maintain.

Culzean Castle
Culzean Castle in Ayrshire is one of Robert Adam's great masterpieces. Between 1777 and 1792 he transformed the 16th century tower house into the present Georgian mansion perched dramatically on the cliff top. Culzean is the Trust's 'flagship' and the transfer of the castle and park to the Trust in association with other public bodies, broke new ground and established working practice and procedures for saving so much of our heritage and traditions. The rehabilitation and redecoration of the interior began in 1972 and continued for twelve years. In each room paint scrapes were taken to ascertain the original colours and we found that Robert Adam used a surprisingly limited palette. On the basis of this colour analysis we then painted a test area in what we believed to be the original colour scheme to see if it 'read' correctly.

Culzean Castle – new carpet in Round Drawing Room.

The Saloon or Round Drawing Room had been decorated as recently as 1968 based on an original Adam watercolour which did not read very happily. We therefore undertook a full investigation and together with the help of the watercolour we determined the original 18th century colour scheme. The plate glass in the windows was removed and correct glazing with astragals was re-instated. Finally a new carpet was made being a copy of the original one. Instead of the flat loop pile which was impossible to have copied, the wool was shot through from the back by a new process and sealed with latex. Visitors can now walk over to the windows to admire the magnificent view down to the Mull of Kintyre.

In the dining room which was formed from the original library and dressing room in 1877, in the

Adamesque style, the decoration was too fussy. The plasterwork had all been picked out in different colours. We decided to paint the whole ceiling in a single colour as it had been originally and this treatment has pulled the room together. The chandelier, designed for acetylene gas, has been fitted with globes and an old oriental carpet has been put down.

On the splendid Oval Staircase, too, we strove to achieve an authentic 18th century effect. All 168 balusters were dismantled, cleaned, redecorated and replaced. For the lighting we had a dozen glass globes blown from a pattern we supplied — a bell-shaped lamp we found in the attic. This work was completed in 1984.

What began as a challenge to save Culzean and to conserve its essential character and atmosphere developed into a determination to provide the stimulus so that visitors of every age and interest could derive intellectual as well as recreational value from their time at Culzean.

The Georgian House
The Georgian House in Charlotte Square, Edinburgh presented us with a different challenge again. The house had been passed to the National Trust for Scotland in satisfaction of death duties but had been let for many years as a smart antique shop. When the lease expired in 1972, we decided to recreate a Georgian professional man's house of the late 18th century, when Charlotte Square was built. We used as

Georgian House – kitchen.

a guide early inventories and sale catalogues, as there was no furniture in the house. We have had to collect appropriate pieces by gift, bequest and purchase and we are still adding to the collection, trying to improve it.

For the drawing room decoration we used a portrait from the Irish National Portrait Gallery of 'Mrs Congreve and her daughters' by Philip Reinagle and we have copied the disposition of the furniture about the perimeter of the room, the pictures hanging above eye level, the carpet in the centre and the fender right across the grate. We have left one case cover on a chair just to show that in the 18th century you only took your covers off when you had distinguished visitors.

In contrast to the drawing room, the parlour is an informal room, a comfortable, Walter Scott style room, where you would sit at a centre table writing letters, reading or sewing.

The kitchen was a real challenge: everything had to be acquired, including all fixtures and fittings. The range was found in a skip and the bread oven underneath the main railway line at East Linton. The collection of utensils has been added to for over 15 years and it has almost become too much of a good thing.

House of Dun
We are currently working on House of Dun, a ravishing Palladian villa of modest size overlooking

House of Dun.

the Montrose Basin. It had degenerated to the status of a hotel, but this was not quite a case of 'Trust or bust'. Mrs Lovat, the last of the family line, wanted the National Trust for Scotland to have the property so that it could be restored, and to this end she gave farms to pay for the necessary work.

Architecturally the house really belongs to two periods: 1730, when the William Adam house with its exuberant plasterwork was built, and the Lady Augusta Fitzclarence period, the 1840s, from which most of the surviving furniture dates. Lady Augusta was the natural daugher of William IV and Mrs Jordan who married John Kennedy Erskine of Dun.

We have undertaken an enormous rehabilitation programme here. Externally we have reinstated the rustication on the south front, restored the glazing bars to the windows and we are putting back the balustrade and urns to crown the façade.

There is a very great deal to do to the interior. As always we began by removing paint and wallpaper to see what had been there originally. The plasterwork in the Saloon by Joseph Enzer is superb but it had all been painted white with a cold blue background. We have now painted it in soft white against a sage green ground and the doors have been oak grained as they originally were.

We have gone to considerable lengths to get the basic details right throughout the house – delightful hob grates had been boarded up and these have now been exposed. Simple cornices have been run in rooms which had never been completed and of course original colour schemes whenever possible have been restored. When the house is completed there will be more to see here than at any other Trust property.

Conclusion
When the National Trust for Scotland takes on a property for whatever reason we take on responsibility for more than the fabric of a building or an acreage of land. We become custodians of the history and traditions that have accumulated in that place. It is our duty to maintain the properties in our care to the highest standards, taking into account the changes that have taken place and above all letting the houses speak for themselves.

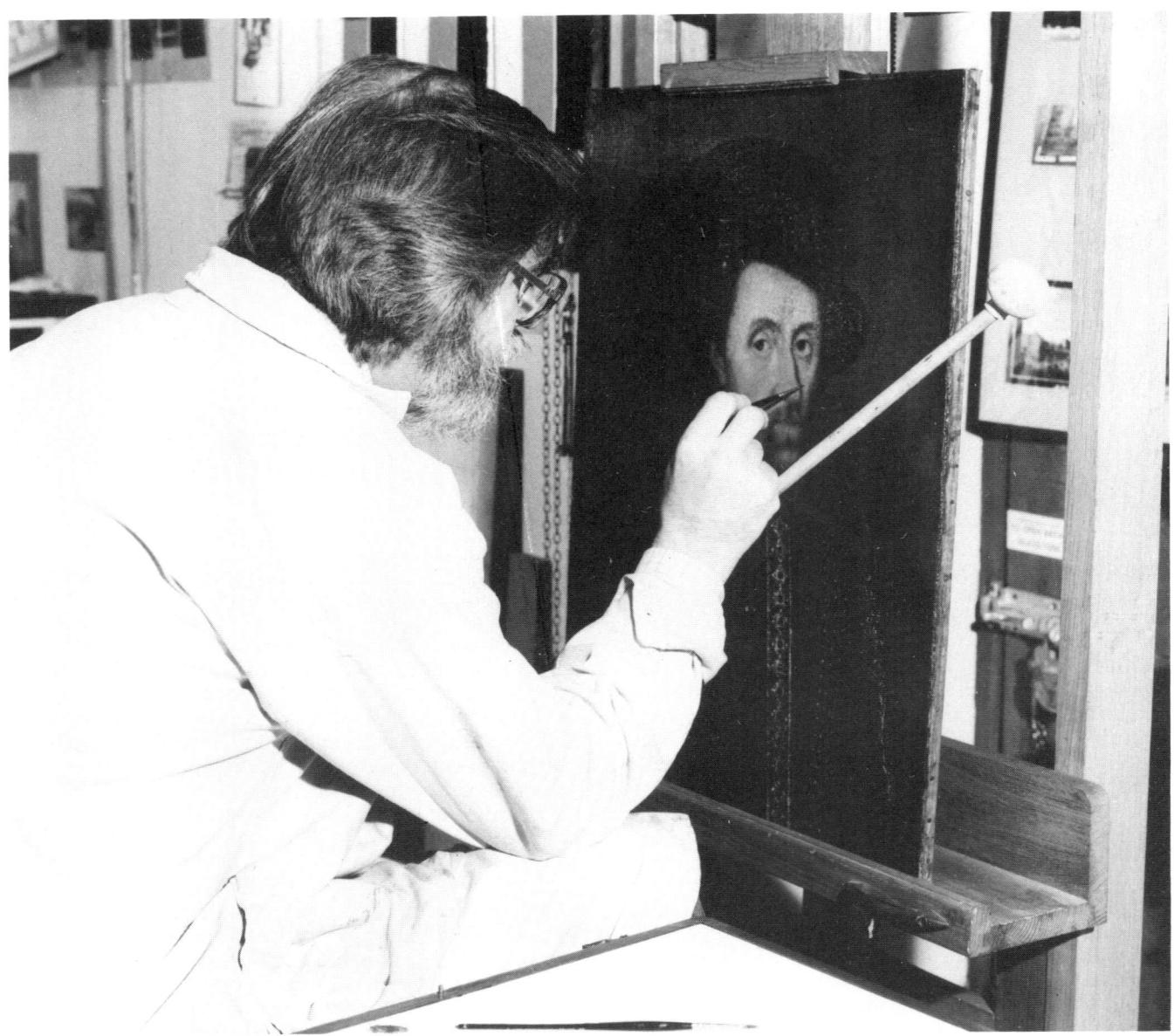

Restoration work on a painting from Dumbarton Castle at Historic Scotland's conservation unit.

PRESENTING·SCOTLAND'S·STORY

THE WORK OF THE HISTORIC BUILDINGS AND MONUMENTS DIRECTORATE

David Connelly

David Connelly has been Director of Historic Buildings and Monuments, Scotland since 1987.

Introduction

The main aim of HBM is the conservation and preservation of buildings, man-made structures and their remains, from the dawn of time to thirty years ago — that being the minimum age for the listing of a building of architectural importance. We also recognise that historic buildings and archaeological remains are interesting and important to the general public, both residents and visitors, and that makes us part of the tourist industry. We are the single biggest provider of visitor attractions in Scotland. The marketing of our estate and the creation of visitor facilities are today additional important tasks; we do this under the title 'Historic Scotland'.

My aim is to give you an account of the range of our work, and to show how these two aims of conservation and of the development of visitor services interact, and how we set about achieving them. I want to explain who we are, what we do, how much of the taxpayer's money we spend, and what we spend it on.

The Staff

Altogether, there are about 630 of us, working full time. In addition, we take on each spring about 75 seasonal staff to supplement the regular custodians at monuments. We are all civil servants on the staff of the Scottish Office, and the work we do is all carried out on behalf of the Secretary of State for Scotland. Just over half of HBM's staff are industrial workers who maintain the monuments in our care, and, as is to be expected, the principal skill is that of the stonemason. The next largest group are the custodians and warders who take your money at the gate, show you round, and keep the sites neat and tidy.

As well as the 100 management and clerical staff, there are about 100 in specialist professional and technical jobs — architects, draughtsmen, quantity surveyors, archaeologists, architectural historians, photographers. There are also 12 uniformed constables at the two Royal parks at Linlithgow and Holyrood, shop assistants at Edinburgh Castle, and a conservation unit at Stenhouse in Edinburgh which can handle easel and wall paintings and stonework.

The Task and Spending on it

The aims of HBM are these:

'To promote on behalf of the Secretary of State the conservation of Scotland's antiquities, monuments, historic buildings and significant parks and gardens of historical interest, and to increase public understanding and enjoyment of them.'

The way in which we realise or approach these aims, and the money spent on them, can be broken down under four main headings.

	Estimated Expenditure 1988-89	
	£m	%
1. Care and maintenance of monuments in care, and of Holyroodhouse.	9.5	44
2. Visitor services (presentation, purchase of merchandise, advertising)	2.5	12
3. Conservation through statutory controls and grants to owners.	8.4	39
4. Rescue archaeology and archaeology at monuments in care.	1.1	5
	21.5	100
Receipts from admissions and sales	2.9	14
Net Government expenditure	18.6	86

These figures include an apportionment of our £7m staff budget.

The largest category of expenditure is on monuments in our care, with grants to owners of historic buildings running a close second. We plan to spend £7.5 million on grants this year, compared with £5.5 million last year — a substantial increase.

Statutory Controls: Listing and Scheduling

Underlying these expenditures are the statutory controls which identify and define our heritage, and form the first line of defence in ensuring that we have a heritage to hand down to posterity. Once a monument is 'scheduled' or a building 'listed', the owner is no longer free to do with it as he wishes. If he wishes to change the features which make it worthy of protection, or to remove it altogether, he must first of all obtain consent from the planning authority or from the Secretary of State, or risk a penalty. This is the common concept behind both 'listing' and 'scheduling' — the different terms coming from different statutes. Broadly speaking, historic buildings are buildings of architectural or historic importance which are inhabited or in use, or are capable of habitation or use. Other structures, or remains of structures, are monuments.

At the moment there are more than 35,000 historic buildings, classified under three qualitative headings.

Category	*Definition*	*No Listed*	*%*
A	Buildings of national importance either of architectural or historical interest	2,468	7
B	Buildings primarily of local importance	23,215	65
C	Good buildings which may have been altered but retain elements of interest; and simple, often traditional, buildings which have group interest.	9,807	28
		35,731*	100

*This includes 241 buildings in East Lothian which have not yet been categorised.

No-one knows for certain just how many 'Ancient

Monuments' we have. It could be anything between 70,000 and perhaps twice that number, because there is no complete catalogue and because new discoveries are being made all the time. There are four broad categories of monuments, of which those in the care or ownership of the Secretaty of State are the first division.

1. Monuments in care	330
2. Scheduled Monuments	4400
3. Monuments of interest and quality, not scheduled	16000
4. Total monuments in Scotland	?70000-140000

Grants to Owners

I described statutory controls as our first line of defence. Our second is a policy of encouragement rather than restraint, represented by the payment of grants to owners of both monuments and buildings. In 1987-88 the grants paid to assist owners in the upkeep of ancient monuments were a modest £95,000.

The distribution of historic building grant in 1987-88 was:

	£'000	%
National Trust for Scotland (NTS)		
— maintenance 223		
— repair works 337	560	10
Individual Owners	1,951	36
Churches	1,496	27
Conservation Areas	1,477	27
Total	5,484	100

Grant is not normally paid towards regular maintenance, and that given to the NTS recognises the heavy burden of the major houses in the Trust's care. Many of the Trust's early acquisitions had little or no endowment. These statutory processes contribute very largely to ensuring that 'Scotland's Story' remains as complete as possible. Were it not for these powers, Scotland's architectural story today would have lost for ever whole chapters which no-one could re-write.

Examples of buildings whose future has been secured by listing, or the prospect of listing, include the following:

> Alva Mill, Clackmannan
> Jute mills in Dundee
> Engine shop at Alexander Stephens & Sons, Linthouse, Glasgow, which is to be dismantled and re-erected at Irvine for use at the Scottish Maritime Museum.
> Thatched houses, being cared for by the Friends of Thatched Houses.

Amongst the leading visitor attractions in our field which we have assisted with Historic Buildings Repair Grant are:

> Glamis Castle
> Inveraray Castle
> Thirlestane Castle
> Dunmore Pineapple
> Rothesay Winter Gardens

In 1987-88, 194 applications for grant were received, and 131 offers were made and accepted; in many cases the work extends over several years, so that at any one time there are many hundreds of active cases being handled.

All these buildings are integral parts of our history, and by aiding their conservation we ensure that the history of our country can be fully presented and understood. Where Historic Building grant is involved we go further, and make public access a condition of the award of grant. The degree of access depends on the historic and architectural interest of the building, and the reasons for its being listed — there is no point in asking for public access to the inside of a building whose only point of interest is its facade.

Public understanding and enjoyment

All of the 330 monuments in our care are open or accessible to the public, except for a few where there are safety considerations. At some 75 of these sites we have a custodian and make a charge for admission, and it is at these where we make our major effort to create an informed public which supports our aims. I want to stress that our general approach is one of conservation, not restoration, and certainly not conjectural restoration. Our aim is to preserve what we find, and I quote with approval some lines of verse by the eminent 19th century architect, Sir George Gilbert Scott

> Beware lest one worn feature ye efface,
> Seek not to add one touch of modern grace;
> Handle with reverence each crumbling stone,
> Respect the very lichen o'er it grown:
> And bid each ancient monument to stand
> Supported e'en as with a filial hand,

Our aim is to work with a 'filial hand', but I would not promise that we respect the 'very lichen' as often the first job on a ruined building is to remove vegetation and have a proper look at the fabric.

Before 1985 we did very little towards increasing public awareness, or towards catering for the enjoyment of visitors to the properties in our care. In mitigation it must also be said that up to that time we had resources of neither manpower nor money to devote to that task.

Today we have a Marketing and Visitor Services Branch which was established with the specific objectives of promoting and publicising our estate, of attracting greater numbers of visitors, and of ensuring that their visits are enjoyable as well as informative experiences. This Branch is also charged with realising the commercial potential of our monuments and maximising revenue. Almost all our properties are now well signposted, and there is a steadily expanding portfolio of free literature telling people what we have to offer, and distributed through a range of channels including Tourist Information Centres, hotels, guesthouses, and so on.

Professionally planned advertising campaigns are run in selected media to reach both tourists and the resident population; we have set up semi-permanent displays in tourist offices; and editorial coverage in all media has increased. All of this has been done with considerable care, for we have been (and still are) acutely conscious of the need to ensure that the 'product' matches the advertising claims. It is absolutely fundamental in our view that the visitor's expectations must be realised, that he goes away feeling, at the very least, that he has had good value for money. To this end we have spent about £0.5 million on the design and the installation of information boards at many of our properties to improve the on-site interpretation and information. This is in addition to the major projects we have completed at Fort George, Jedburgh, Edzell, and most

The exhibition area in the award-winning visitor centre at Jedburgh Abbey.

recently, at the Dallas Dhu Distillery near Forres. All have been the subject of special promotional campaigns, and in all cases the results have been satisfactory. Improved presentation and energetic promotion can have considerable impact on visitor numbers at even such a small property as Edzell Castle, where there was an increase from 7,500 in 1986 to nearly 12,000 in 1987.

Even more dramatic is the impact on income which comes from attracting high numbers of visitors, and introducing a well-designed and well-stocked visitor centre-cum-sales point. At Fort George sales are expected to be £28,500 this year, as against £7,500 in 1986. At Edzell — where the investment was very modest — trading income rose from £711 in 1986 to £3,704 in 1987.

An interesting result of these developments has been the changing relationship between Edinburgh Castle

The interior of the visitor centre at Edzell Castle.

and the rest of the estate. Edinburgh will always be our flagship — and I will have more to say about the Castle later — and has for years accounted for about half our total number of visitors and 80 per cent of our trading income. But we now see a trend towards Edinburgh being slightly less dominant, with other monuments jointly contributing a growing share of the total. The expectation for 1988 is that we will log a total of some 2.15 million visitors, of which 957,000 will visit Edinburgh Castle.

On retail trading, returns so far indicate that we can expect to have a turnover of £1 million for the first time. Edinburgh's contribution to this will be in the region of £760,000.

We have also been at work transforming our guidebooks to make them more visually attractive and readable publications. We have established Friends of the Scottish Monuments, and now have some 22,000 members, of whom about 1200 are life members. We are also about to give our custodians new and more welcoming uniforms — the prison officer style uniforms they have worn for so long do not present a friendly image to the visitor.

Links with the tourist industry and the travel trade have been developed. One result of this was the introduction of our 'Explorer' tickets. These are sold on commission by Area Tourist Boards and travel agents, and give the visitor free access to all monuments for 7 or 14 days for a single concessionary payment. The Monuments management side of HBM today is very commercially conscious. We have a commercial sponsor in the shape of Gateway Foodmarkets, whose support has allowed us to appoint an Education Officer. But I assure you that nothing we have so far done, or have planned for the future, is at the expense of the 'historical integrity' of the estate.

Perhaps a better way to express that would be to say that in addition to preserving and conserving Scotland's built heritage we are increasingly conscious that we must present it well whenever we can. This may involve us in co-operative ventures with other organisations, and sometimes in handing over a finished project for someone else to promote and to use.

Two Cases in More Detail:

Chatelherault
An outstanding recent example of a co-operative venture is the restoration of Chatelherault, the principal surviving building from the estate of the Dukes of Hamilton. This was an exception to what I said earlier about restoration, but it was not a conjectural restoration, as there was firm evidence for all that we did there.

In 1732 the 5th Duke of Hamilton commissioned William Adam to design a terminal building for the south end of a three-mile avenue in his park. This was to act as an eye-catcher, as well as a kennel for his hounds, but by the time the job was completed in 1743 the brief had expanded to include a dining room and other apartments, all finished by the best craftsmen in Scotland. The building was called Chatelherault, after a French title bestowed on the Hamilton who was second Earl of Arran. The family fortunes declined in the 19th century, and in 1927 Hamilton Palace was demolished. By the 1970s all that remained was the family mausoleum and a derelict Chatelherault.
When the Secretary of State for Scotland acquired Chatelherault in 1978 in order to save it for the nation it had been abandoned for a number of years. Vandalism, and a series of fires, had caused roofs and floors to collapse; only fragments of the fine plasterwork and carved woodwork remained. The brave and bold decision was taken to restore the lodge and the surrounding parkland. We took on the lodge, and Strathclyde RC and Hamilton DC, with Countryside Commission and European Community help, took on the park and landscape.

Our first task was to stabilise the outer shell, for

which the local quarry was re-opened to provide the original stone. Simultaneously, old archive material and surviving fragments were being studied to obtain as much information as possible about the interiors. The result was such a complete picture that it was decided to renew them. Architects had to translate old and sometimes blurred photographs into measured drawings, and master craftsmen in plaster work, woodcarving and carpentry had to reproduce exact replicas of the originals. In the dining room, fragments of a fireplace surround were found to be of 'Cambuslang Marble' — a locally quarried material no longer available. Persistent detective work led to an old coal tip where sufficient pieces were found to form a new surround.

While all of this was going on, Hamilton District Council was building and equipping a visitor centre, and the formal garden was being revived. The restored Chatelherault was formally opened by the

A view of the restored Chatelherault and of the re-planted formal garden.

Duke of Gloucester last year, and is now the focal point of Hamilton District's Country Park; we have handed over the management of the lodge to the district council. The total cost of the whole project was just over £6.7 million, of which the Secretary of State's share was about £3 million. This may seem a lot, but it is the price for the restoration and preservation of a major work of art. It is now back in use, but I believe that Chatelherault is important in itself; its day to day use is a bonus.

Edinburgh Castle
While all the presentation projects at Jedburgh, Fort George and other sites have been going on, there has been one site which has been a constant concern. Edinburgh Castle attracts about 1 million visitors a year; it is one of the top three or four tourist attractions in Britain; and it is central to the story of Scotland's history. Yet we have been acutely conscious that the standard of presentation and of visitor facilities in general has been below an acceptable level. Our paying customers had a right to expect something very much better from one of the most famous castles in the world. The Tattoo presents us with particular problems, because it occupies the Esplanade from June to early October, during all the peak months for visitors. But we concluded there was nothing to be done. To try to remove the Tattoo to a new site was unthinkable, although the management of the Castle would be easier without its presence there.

The decision that something should be done to improve matters was the easy part. Much more tricky was deciding just what we should do. Whatever scheme was to be implemented had to satisfy the expectations of our visitors, had to be acceptable to the people of Scotland, had to be historically correct and economically viable, and also had to meet the reasonable requirements of our 'tenants' — the Army and the Scottish United Services Museum and so on.

Three years of consultations and deliberations produced the scheme which the Secretary of State announced in April of this year. Following consultation with the Army and the National Museums there is to be a reallocation and rearrangement of accommodation within the Castle.

The main change will be that the Scottish United Services Museum will be concentrated in the former 'hospital square' at the north west of the Castle. As a consequence, HBM will have for the first time full control of the principal buildings of the Castle around Crown Square. We will use that control to offer a proper interpretation of the history of the buildings, of the Stuart monarchy, and of the Honours of Scotland. I am very pleased that the National Galleries and the National Museums have agreed to help us in this work.

The physical comfort of our visitors will be helped by our providing a café, where our shop is now. The shop, already inadequate, will move to a larger space nearer the gatehouse. Also in that area there will be improved lavatories. The most expensive part of the work, a vehicle and services tunnel, will be the least obtrusive. It will enable us to separate pedestrian and vehicle traffic — there are 7000 or so pedestrians each way on peak summer days. It will also provide a new and better route for the Castle's outdated services — gas, electricity, water and telephones.

Early in December the contract will be awarded for Phase I — tunnel, new shop and lavatories. Work on site will start in December, and should be completed by the end of 1989. It will be well into the 1990s before the rest of the programme will be finished, mainly because so many of the accommodation moves are consequential. I am confident that by the mid 1990s Edinburgh Castle will be a much more interesting and comfortable place to visit than it is now. One new feature in the later phases will be accommodation for groups visiting the Castle, including a classroom.

Looking to the Future
Although Edinburgh Castle will be absorbing a very large share of our resources for the next 7 or 8 years, I would not like you to think that the rest of our estate will be neglected. Far from it. We have a programme of development work at monuments which will take us well into the 'nineties. At Stirling Castle there will be a major improvement to on-site interpretation, including the opening up of some new areas to visitors, and work on the rehabilitation of the major buildings and apartments, including the Great Hall, after three centuries of military use, will continue; at St Andrews, we have bought more land beside the Castle where we intend to build a new visitor centre which will tell the story of both Castle and Cathedral in the history of St Andrews and of Scotland; Inchcolm — the island in the Firth of Forth and site of an Augustinian priory — was used by the forces in the two world wars, and will be the site of a permanent exhibition covering all aspects of the Firth's wartime role; we have plans for Orkney, beginning with improving access, creating a visitor centre and promoting the splendid (but presently under-visited) Broch of Gurness, and with improvements in mind also near Maeshowe. Caerlaverock Castle in Dumfriesshire, Melrose Abbey, Rothesay Castle, Doune Castle, Tantallon Castle, Linlithgow Palace, — these and others are all in line for varying degrees of presentational and promotional improvement.

We know what we want to do, and I think that our record over the past few years proves that we know how to do it. All we need is the resources, for certainly the will and the ability are there to present our buildings and monuments as vital and fascinating parts of Scotland's story.

As I see things now, I do not expect any startling changes. We intend to build on the successful experience of the past 3/4 years. We want to build up the Friends, and perhaps to join with them in some more positive aspect of our enterprise. The Government has said that we are to be an executive agency. That will not in itself affect our policies and plans but I hope we shall be more free to follow our own ideas. We want to use our participation in tourism in a positive way, for the benefit of our main task of conserving the nation's buildings and monuments. We want also to use our participation in tourism for the benefit of Scots and Scotland, by helping to increase both understanding and prosperity.

Rows of axeheads and swords at the National Museum of Antiquities of Scotland, ca 1890.

SCOTLAND'S HISTORY IN THE NATIONAL MUSEUMS OF SCOTLAND

Robert Anderson

Robert Anderson, Director of the National Museums of Scotland since 1984, first worked in the Royal Museum of Scotland as Assistant Keeper in 1970-1975, before moving to the Science Museum. He is President of the British Society for the History of Science and has published widely on the history of science and museology.

Preparing papers for conferences can often be a salutory experience, with the simplest sounding themes often proving to be the most complex. 'The Role of the Museum' in Presenting Scotland's Story may seem to be straightforward. It is probably true to say that every museum in Scotland is involved to some degree or other in Presenting Scotland's Story. But, on reflection, it is also probably the case that no museum has been established specifically with this aim in mind. At present, no single museum provides anything approaching a comprehensive view, or even a coherent, balanced story of part of it. For the fact is that museums are set up for reasons other than this and their ambitions are different: museums funded by district councils usually concentrate on local history; university museums often reflect the collecting, research and teaching interests of their staff; independent industrial museums concern themselves with specific industries which have been conducted in the past at particular sites; regimental museums speak for themselves. No museum has presented a national history in Scotland or, indeed, in the United Kingdom.

There are a number of approaches that could be adopted in tackling this difficult, open-ended subject. For example, the efforts which are being made by Scottish museums could be surveyed and the strengths and weaknesses in the overall picture identified; or the question of how a nation might choose to present itself through the medium of the museum might be considered; or again, the benefits and disadvantages of the chronological versus thematic approach could be discussed.

In fact, this paper will start to tackle something more fundamental, examining the relationship between an assemblage of objects in a museum and a country's history. It becomes increasingly clear that while objects can illuminate certain, but by no means all, aspects of history, they cannot tell a historical narrative by themselves. They need very sophisticated interpretations by the visitor, who may or may not understand the process which he is taking himself through. But in addition to a theoretical approach, the opportunity will be taken at the end of this paper to discuss how the National

Museums of Scotland hopes to tackle the problem of presenting its artefacts and natural objects in a new Museum to present Scotland's Story — if it is given half a chance to do so.

Throughout their period of development, from the late Renaissance to the present, museums have been established for a wide variety of reasons. Some have been more focused in their intent than others, and some have clear statements of their aims and objectives from their foundation. But these would seem to be in the minority. Efforts to compile such statements often result in extremely general and unuseful generalisations. Early museums, which did not consider public needs as carefully as we do today, could have sharper ambitions.

The earliest collections to which the public were admitted, the princely collections of curiosities, jewels and art, were clearly not intended to tell a story, or illuminate history. They were intended to be a reflection of the power at the disposal of their owner, or of his intellectual qualities *(Impey and MacGregor, 1985)*. The first truly public museum in the British Isles, that donated by Elias Ashmole to the University of Oxford, was accompanied by a statement of its extremely practical purpose:

> 'Because the knowledge of Nature is very necessarie to humaine life, health, & the conveniences thereof, & because that knowledge cannot so soe well & usefully attain'd, except the history of Nature be knowne & considered; and to this is requisite the inspection of Particulars, especially those as are extraordinary in their Fabrick, or useful in Medicine, or applyed to Manufacture or Trade.' *(Welch, 1983).*

Early museums such as Ashmole's contained complete cross-sections of museum objects of their day. Until the end of the 19th century, the British Museum in Bloomsbury exhibited natural history collections alongside classical antiquities; and of course, many museums still do, the Royal Museum of Scotland included.

All museums collect objects to ensure their preservation: this is a fundamental activity. Without the existence of a group of objects whose long-term future is secured, nothing else can follow. However the uses to which collections may be put thereafter can be very diverse. Some collections may be reserved for scholarly research, others may have an overtly educational function, whilst other categories may be exploited to reinforce strong statements which curators wish to make.

It is clear that the Scottish national collections, those of the former National Museum of Antiquities of Scotland and Royal Scottish Museum, which were amalgamated in October 1985 to form the National Museums of Scotland, were developed for very different purposes.[1]

By 1985, the National Museum of Antiquities had been in existence for 205 years, the Royal Scottish Museum for 131 years. Each had developed a distinct tradition of its own which closely reflected the original purpose for its foundation. Each, in its own way, presented material which reflected aspects of Scottish history and prehistory. Because the traditions are still apparent in today's museums in Queen Street and Chambers Street, it is of interest to know how these distinct presentation methods arose, and in which way they can inform our present day views on how we should deal with future exhibitions.

One obvious difference is that the National Museum of Antiquities of Scotland was established by a learned Society, the Society of Antiquaries of Scotland, and the Royal Scottish Museum was established by government, the Department of Science and Art. The sponsoring bodies stamped their marks clearly on the museums.

The Society of Antiquaries was established in 1780, and one impetus for this development was the feeling that important material had been neglected. Major collections formed by Sir Andrew Balfour and Sir Robert Sibbald had been bequeathed to the University of Edinburgh, but had been dispersed during the course of the 18th century. In 1782, William Smellie wrote his account of the institution of the Society, recording:

> 'An association similar to the Antiquarian Society of London was projected by several gentlemen of eminence and learning, some of whom had made private collections, and were anxious that these, and others which they knew to be scattered through the country, should be preserved in a secure and permanent repository. . . . They considered that some useful materials, which had been amassed by interested Antiquaries, were now perishing in the possession of persons who knew not their values.'

The objects acquired by the antiquaries were not intended for public exhibition, and in this way the museum differed from the British Museum in London which had been established in 1753. The objects acquired were for preservation and for research. Many of the early papers of the Society's *Transactions* are concerned with objects in the collections and their interpretation. Housing the objects was a continuous concern and to begin with they were kept in the Antiquaries' 'large and commodious' hall near the Cowgate, from January 1781.

The collection, like the Society, was peripatetic for the first fifty years of its existence. Collecting was spasmodic. In 1821, William Brewster referred to the coin collection as 'subjects of antiquity . . . when collected together supply a very valuable record of ancient manners and history, offering facilities to antiquarian research. . . .' Brewster also refers to series of coins as 'evidence of ancient history.' Perhaps this is the first time that the collection is referred to in terms of its value to the understanding of history.

The first really public view of the collection came after the move to the Royal Institution on the Mound in 1826, when cases were constructed for the 'various interesting and highly valuable articles of the museum'. The curator, James Skene, at the Anniversary Meeting that year, reviewed the history of the Society's collections and remarked:

> 'On the Continent there is scarcely a town of any note that cannot boast of an establishment in full activity, where local Antiquities are accurately investigated with a view to the elucidation of history. . . . With us, on the contrary, objects of curiosity and interest are not infrequently assigned to dusty garrets, where they are as little useful to their owners as satisfactory to the public.'

Then, pleading for donations, Skene said:

> 'Monuments obviously intended by some former race of inhabitants as historical memorials to their posterity are to be found in every quarter of the country, and many more have been destroyed under our eyes.'

It seems clear that Skene was seeing the importance of artefacts for the elucidation of history by antiquarian research. The collection as exhibited did not tell the history without intervening interpretation by the cognoscenti.

However this attitude to objects and their historical significance created a clearer *story* than could be achieved at the sister museum established in 1854, the Industrial Museum of Scotland, where the initial intention was rather different. Its aims were quite clearly stated in its Directory of 1858:

> 'The Industrial Museum of Scotland is . . . a Museum of the Industry of the world in special relation to Scotland . . . it embodies, like the similar Museums in the country, a fourfold idea:

Exhibitional galleries, where the raw, workable, and accessory materials on which Industrial Art is exercised; the tools and machines employed to modify these; and the finished products resulting from their modification, including the various stages of progress between the original material and the perfect products are systematically arranged,' *(Anon, 1858)*.

The other three parts of the 'idea' were a laboratory, library and lecture series.

The Industrial Museum was, therefore, restricted in ambition and strongly didactic in style. Never was there an intention to tell Scotland's story, except in the narrowest of senses.

Thus, examining the two precursors of the National Museums of Scotland in the mid-19th century, it becomes apparent that it would then have been impossible to begin to portray a national history, not only because the collections were in an embryo state of development, but because the two rather rigid museums' philosophies restricted the breadth of collecting.

What has happened since that time? Perhaps not as much as might be thought. It has already been suggested, the stories the two parent institutions tell, even today, are distinctive in style. The two museums deal with different subjects, and it is obvious that the conclusions that can be drawn from a careful examination of neolithic beakers are different in nature from those which result from study of a line of steam engines. In part, of course, it is because considerable supplementary information on the latter is available in the form of documentary material and published works. Given the choice of studying only artefacts or only literary sources to elucidate the history of the industrial revolution, all historians would choose the archives and books — and they would be very sensible to do so. For the study of neolithic man, there is no choice.

It is worth attempting to analyse the two museums. On the ground floor of the old National Museum of Antiquities of Scotland are the sculptured stones. Because of space constraints, they are displayed in a way which makes them look like a fossil forest. What do they tell the average, or even well-educated visitor about the Story of Scotland? Obviously by themselves, very little indeed. The labels describe the stones and their carvings but do not generate a story of any coherence. There is no implied criticism whatsoever of the curator or designer: it is just that the artefacts themselves are limited in their ability on their own to tell stories to the ordinary visitor. There can be no doubt whatsoever that these stones mean a considerable amount to the scholar; but then he is using the stones to stimulate his background knowledge, which has been formed by the bringing together of many pieces of evidence which he has absorbed in his studies. Certainly we could 'interpret' the stones by text and by the use of graphic images, so that they would mean considerably more than by the use of minimal labelling. But it would be the 'book on the wall' which would be telling the story.

Rows of sculptured stones at the Royal Museum of Scotland (formerly the National Museum of Antiquities of Scotland), 1988.

Until relatively recently, little effort was made to assist the visitor in museums. Collections of objects were displayed using a taxonomic approach as in traditional study collections of insects. When photographs of the National Museum of Antiquities when it was in the Royal Institution in the 1880s are examined the approach becomes very apparent. Some might even smile at the naivety and lack of sophistication of the curators of the day. But this would be dangerous, and if our current displays of the same material at Queen Street are examined a major change of approach will not be clearly seen. The archaeological evidence itself is being presented in a stark, straightforward manner rather than an attempt being made to tell a story to the public.

There have been recent attempts to present prehistoric material in other ways. Perhaps notable was David Clarke's exhibition 'Symbols of Power' at York Buildings in Edinburgh in 1985. *(Clarke, Cowie and Foxon, 1985)*. This was an exhibition which aimed to provide a context for objects which were defined as prestige possessions. To quote directly from the publicity material, itself an important aid to interpretation, 'We hope to encourage you to see prehistoric people not as squat grunting savages but as people with aims and aspirations not unlike our own, whose ideas of power and prestige in their time have much to say about power and prestige in the 1980s.' The stance taken by the curator was, of course, much debated by the archaeological fraternity, perhaps because of the uncompromising approach. I imagine that the objects made a greater impression on the average visitor than the straightforward taxonomic mode of display, because he or she was encouraged to adopt a particular view in which to judge the re-exhibited collection. However, the way in which objects were exhibited stopped short of the presentation of a story.

The didactic approach of Chambers Street can also be examined. There are no actual photographs of visitors examining the collections in the 19th century, but there is an informative woodcut from Grant's *Old and New Edinburgh of 1882*. (Is it significant that in surviving 19th century illustrations of the National Museum of Antiquities of Scotland it is the scholarly curators who are shown with the collection, while in the Royal Scottish Museum it is the thronging public?) Here the visitors are clearly engaged in a learning experience. Lighthouses are being closely

The Royal Scottish Museum in 1882. Visitors (bottom right) scrutinise lighthouses.

scrutinised and doubtless the visitor is being encouraged to understand the principle of the Fresnel lens and the manufacture of flint glass. It is unlikely, however, that the public is being told about the economic impact of improving safety at sea by means of lighthouses, or the social conditions of lighthousemen on a remote island. This is what would be necessary, of course, to start to present a story: and yet this approach is more difficult in terms of the display of objects alone, and perhaps simply not possible. In the historic period there are many different stories to be told with the help of objects. Take lighthouses, for example. Trade and the social conditions of those who work in them has been mentioned. But the story of the Stevenson family who built many of the Scottish lighthouses, the establishment and working arrangements of the Northern Lighthouse Board, the effect of the development of the first DC generators, and what that led to, are all possible approaches to presentation. It all depends on which mission is chosen, and results in the realisation that objects do not mean anything simple and straightforward and the story presented depends on curatorial decisions.

The tradition of the Industrial Museum remains today, as can be seen in the Victorian Engineering hall. Rows of machines can be discovered which are clearly meant to indicate the skill and versatility of the Scottish engineer, in addition to the skill of the museum model makers. This hall was set up as recently as the late 1970s. Nearby in the Hall of Power (the title itself indicates the nuts and bolts approach) stands a slightly more interpreted row of

The taxonomy of the steam engine: the Royal Museum of Scotland (formerly the Royal Scottish Museum) in 1988.

steam engines with graphic back-up material giving an internalist view of their development. But no effort is made to tell the story of the industrial revolution in Scotland. If the visitor already knows about the industrial revolution and the influence (or possibly non-influence) of steam engines, then he will be able to put them into some sort of context. But otherwise he may go away knowing only a little more about the mechanics of the steam engine. Almost certainly little knowledge of industrialisation and urbanisation will be imparted.

A good deal of thought has, on occasions, been put into how to present an historical account by means of exhibited objects. Here I would like to mention an exhibition called 'A Hot Bed of Genius' which was also displayed at York Buildings, this time in 1986.[2] The ambition of the exhibition was to tell the story of the Scottish Enlightenment in a popular way. It was an obvious subject to choose and perhaps at the early stage seemed straightforward. But the process of development of the exhibition was somewhat agonising. Eventually four major figures were chosen

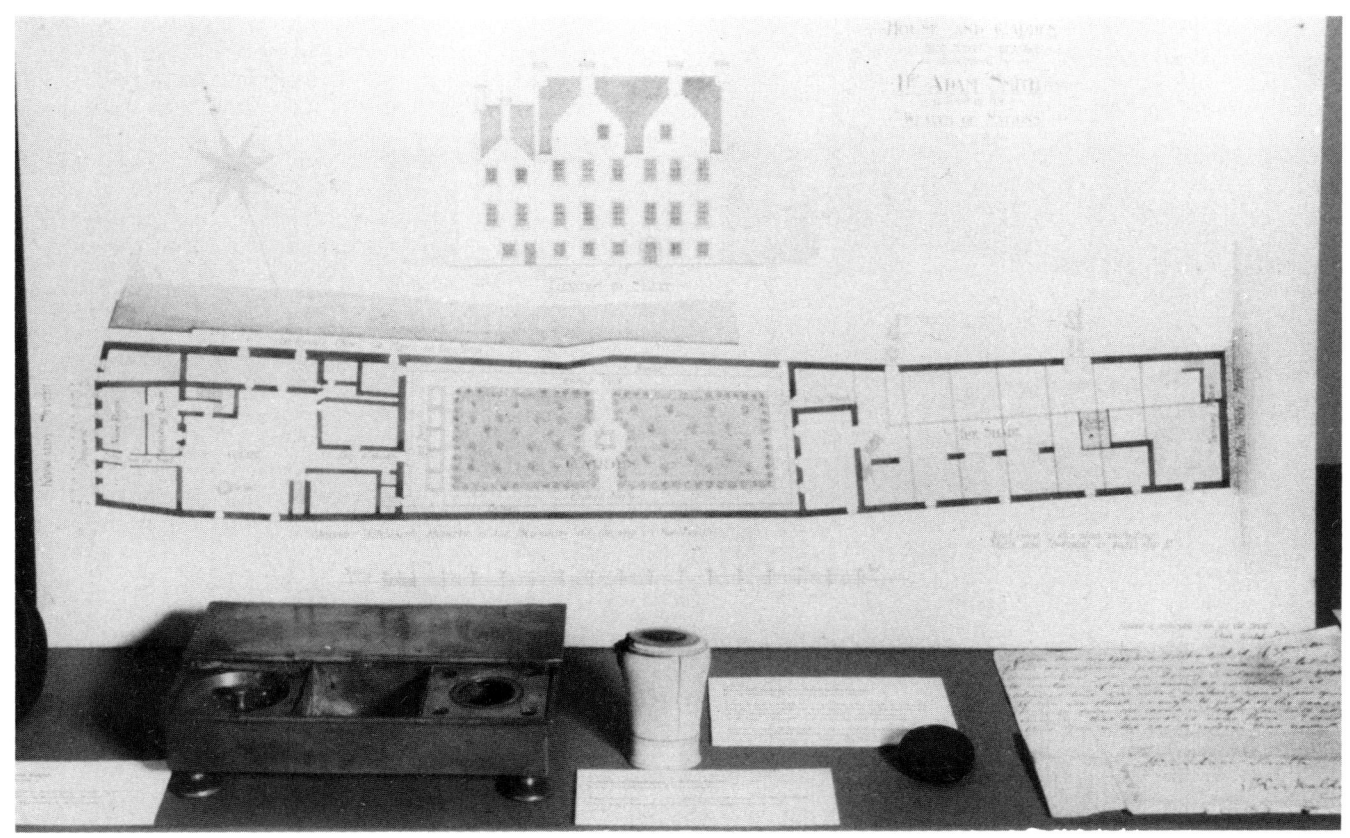

Display on Adam Smith in 'A Hot Bed of Genius' in 1986: personalia and memorabilia, but no economic theory.

to represent the intellectual community of the period: David Hume, Adam Smith, Joseph Black and James Hutton. But clearly there are going to be problems in an exhibition on this theme central to Scottish history: how does one present Hume's views on causation, Smith's economic theory or even Black's work on latent heat? The exhibition itself developed as a series of portraits, memorabilia and personalia, backed up by the books which dealt with these intangible matters. It was an excellent experience, but again, the well-prepared scholar would derive considerably more from it than the curious but uninformed member of the public.

The point has been reached where the National Museums of Scotland plans for their presentation of Scotland's Story in the future can be revealed in outline. The scheme is to build a new museum for the Scottish collections on the corner of Chambers Street in Edinburgh, adjacent to the building originally constructed in 1861 for the Industrial Museum of Scotland. This site was earmarked for a new museum building for the National Museums of Antiquities of Scotland in the 1960s, the proposal being dropped at the last moment in 1976 to facilitate public spending cuts. At present our main Scottish collections on display are those of the former National Museum of Antiquities, which occupy the same totally inadequate 850 square metres which they did when the museum was opened in Queen Street in 1891.

The major intention is to show a much broader view of Scotland than is presently possible, through the medium of the collections and not by the use of either massive graphic texts or by conjectural reconstruction of the Jorvik genre. Our very great strength is our collections, and it is the objects themselves that must be presented. It is planned to provide a coherence which is currently lacking in many museums but which can be achieved by the National Museums of Scotland because of the breadth and depth of the material. The resulting experience will not be balanced history, but that part of the history of Scotland and the Scottish people that can be illuminated by its material culture and natural objects.

We intend to provide approaches which are both chronological and typological. The main, and more popular, thread will be a fairly interdisciplinary presentation which, in a chronological sequence, will relate to aspects of Scottish history. It will be accessible to nearly all of the public, will be presented with a certain lightness of touch, and yet will be a serious but enjoyable experience. The other approach will allow the depth of the collection to be displayed. Off the central spine will be relatively small galleries stuffed with objects of a particular type of manufacture. We might deal with the 19th century potteries, with clocks and watches, or with the Scottish system of weights and measures. It is not expected that more than a proportion of visitors will come to see these galleries, and certainly they should not all be tackled on one visit. But it is surprising how many letters of complaint a director receives about the lack of bagpipes on exhibition. As it happens, we have at least 15 sets displayed at the moment, but some of our friendly pressure groups will not be satisfied until the very last warped chanter finds its place in a case![4] In truth, museum staff are delighted that such enthusiasts abound. The displays themselves will be backed up by a well-stocked information centre where visitors will be encouraged to discover things for themselves and it is hoped to give access to data on our research collections by computer. The wonderful resources of the library will also be made accessible. Other kinds of backup will also be available: educational services will continually be developed, especially courses for school teachers, so that school visits are made more valuable. Publications are also important, and more volumes in our *Spotlight* series will be published which relate the Scottish collections to historical themes for secondary school children. At a more advanced level, we shall continue to co-publish *Review of Scottish Culture,* which has just reached its fourth volume.[5]

This scheme is different from our current

presentation in other ways (apart from occupying ten times the space available at present in Queen Street). The first galleries will deal with non-human aspects. The pre-1985 organisation of the national museums meant that all the geology and zoology of Scotland was at Chambers Street, while most of the artefacts were at Queen Street. The geological and natural history context for the development of Scottish culture in the new display will be provided. Secondly the boundaries between Scotland and the rest of the world will not be drawn as tightly as at present. It is undeniable that Scots have gone forth with their culture all over the world, and also that Scotland has had a changing and developing culture as peoples moved into Scotland from outside. Currently Vikings are dealt with in some detail at Queen Street, but more recent movements of Italians, Poles, Pakistanis, or, dare I say it, the English, are not considered. Which leads on to the third change. Scottish culture presently portrayed would seem to be one third prehistoric, one third Roman and one third mediaeval and Renaissance. Scotland seems to come to an abrupt end in 1850 and is totally non-industrialised; there were no poorer classes, only those who poured tea out of silver teapots or who wore voluminous silk dresses.

What I am saying, of course, is that a better balance, chronologically, culturally and socially must be attempted. There is the potential to achieve this, now that the museums have combined their collection and curatorial resources. In June 1989 the Scottish collections will be presented in a large temporary exhibition called 'The Wealth of a Nation'. This is intended to show the quality, the depth and the potential of our material as a major, underused resource. It will not be a sub-section of the proposed Museum of Scotland but it is to be hoped that everyone will be clamouring for a new museum building by the end of the exhibition when, regretfully, the objects will be returned to their usual displays or to store.

If there is one message I hope I have been able to put to you, it is that Presenting a Story is a complex business requiring great thought, sensitivity and, moreover, an understanding of our public and the way they think. If presenting Scotland's Story seems to be a straightforward matter in your Museum, then it is probably not being dealt with very well.

Bibliography
Anon 1858 *Directory of the Industrial Museum of Scotland, and of the Natural History Museum, Edinburgh* (Science and Art Department of the Committee of Council on Education: London, 1858)
Clarke, D V Cowie, T G and *Foxon, A (1985) Symbols of Power at the Time of Stonehenge* (National Museum of Antiquities of Scotland: Edinburgh).
Impey, O and MacGregor, A (eds), 1985 *The Origins of Museums* (Clarendon Press: Oxford).
Welch, M 1983 'The Foundation of the Ashmolean Museum' in Arthur Macgregor (ed) *Tradescant's Rarities* (Clarendon Press: Oxford).

Footnotes
1 The best history of the National Museum of Antiquities of Scotland is found in two articles by R B K Stevenson in A S Bell (ed.) *The Scottish Antiquarian Tradition* (John Donald, Edinburgh: 1981). There is no adequate history of the Royal Scottish Museum, but see *The Royal Scottish Museum 1854 – 1954* (Oliver and Boyd, Edinburgh, 1954).
2 There is no catalogue as such of this exhibition, though an object list was published by the Institute for Advanced Studies in the Humanities, University of Edinburgh: *A Hotbed of Genius: The Scottish Enlightenment 1730 – 1790. Checklist of Objects* . . . See also D Daiches, P Jones and J Jones *A Hotbed of Genius* (Edinburgh University Press, Edinburgh: 1986).
3 By the end of 1988, nearly all the archaeological records, some 110,000 of them, had been accessioned by the National Museums of Scotland computer, NAPIER
4 This is not a hypothetical case — see *The Observer*, Scotland section, 18 December 1988, 'Sour Notes in Music Row'.
5 Four *Spotlight* packs were published in 1986: *Corn Rigs and Barley Rigs, If it Wasnae for the Weaver, Not Just Haggis* and *Polar Scots*. The *Review of Scottish Culture,* published annually from 1985, is edited by Alexander Fenton, Hugh Cheape and Rosalind K Marshall and is co-published with John Donald Ltd.

National Gallery of Scotland.

SCOTLAND'S HISTORY AT THE NATIONAL GALLERIES

Timothy Clifford

Timothy Clifford has been Director of the National Galleries of Scotland since 1984. He has long experience of museum practice having worked in the Victoria and Albert Museum, the British Museum and as director of Manchester City Art Gallery. He has published extensively in art history.

Exhibitions

I hope that it is very apparent what the National Galleries are doing to tell the story of Scotland. Certainly over the last few years exhibitions entirely devoted to things Scottish have been held at the National Gallery, National Portrait Gallery and the National Gallery of Modern Art. Take for example the exhibitions 'Living off the Land' and the 'Tribute to Wilkie' exhibition at the National Gallery, or 'The Queen's World' and 'The Queen's Image' at the Portrait Gallery, the 'Peploe' exhibition or 'The Vigorous Imagination' at the Gallery of Modern Art. For 1989 we are mounting a major retrospective of William MacTaggart at the Royal Scottish Academy for the Edinburgh International Festival and an important survey of Scottish 20th Century Art at the Gallery of Modern Art.

Acquisitions

During the last decade we have also acquired a large number of Scottish works of art. Our most recent delight is the superb full length portrait by Daniel Mytens of the *3rd Marquis of Hamilton* 1629 which was bought from the present Duke of Hamilton and hangs in the Portrait Gallery in Queen Street. Strikingly posed against blue curtains he is dressed from top to toe in cloth of silver. There is also the grand tenebrist canvas by Sir David Wilkie of *The Finding of the body of Tippu Sahib by Sir David Baird* which contrasts with the much more homely, solid group of the Bethune-Morison Family, an earlier work by the same artist, and the vast picture by Benjamin West of *Alexander III King of Scots saved from the fury of a stag by the intrepid intervention of Colin Fitzgerald*.

The Mound collections have been greatly enhanced by Scottish acquisitions in particular made by Dr. Lindsay Errington who is the Assistant Keeper responsible for this element of the collections. For 1989 she has been appointed Slade Professor of Fine Art at Cambridge and the special lecture theme she has chosen is *The Past in the Present: Paintings and Literature in Scotland in the 19th Century*.

Daniel Mytens: The 3rd Marquis of Hamilton
Scottish National Portrait Gallery.

Purchase Grant

The National Galleries of Scotland have a purchase grant of £1.6 million. How can we add to our collections appropriately? Great old masters are fetching £20 to £30 million, while £8 to £10 million for modern international works of art has become the norm. At the National Galleries we are meant to be curating a Tate Gallery equivalent in Scotland, and equivalents of the combined Print Rooms of the Victoria and Albert Museum and the British Museum while the parallel for photographic collections is the combined collections of the V and A and the National Portrait Gallery in London. We also boast the largest collection of sculpture in Scotland. In this context the sum of £1.6 million for acquiring paintings, sculpture, photographs, watercolours, drawings, and prints for the Scottish nation is hopelessly inadequate. In 1985 we introduced a separate purchase grant for Scottish paintings and Scottish photographs.

Aid to other Scottish Organisations

We have particular obligations on behalf of the Scottish nation. For example, we help the National Trust for Scotland and the Historic Houses Association with the care and documentation of their collections, and we run a photographic survey of pictures in private houses. We have iconographic indices of our photographic collections in the Portrait Gallery. We are also always ready to help and advise museums and galleries throughout Scotland on academic and conservation matters, and we advise for fine art acquisitions on all applications for purchase grants with Government grant-in-aid. Estate Office valuations are also undertaken by the staff on behalf of H.M. Treasury.

We are also avidly collecting the works of living Scots. After the 'Vigorous Imagination' in 1987 we bought a very good collection of works by Bellany, a range of pictures by Steven Campbell, Adrian Wiszniewski, Ken Currie, Gwen Hardie, Stephen Conroy, and a lovely group of prints by Peter Howson. We will continue to collect voraciously the work of Scottish artists of the past and present. The Portrait Gallery also regularly commissions images of celebrated Scots.

Staffing

All that is done at the National Galleries is achieved with a small staff, some 147 members in all, of whom the majority are warding staff, and a very small element devoted to conservation and curatorial work. The education department which you might expect to be comparable with the huge organisation at Glasgow Museums and Art Gallery has just been doubled. We now have two members of staff. The entire staffing and running costs are in the order of £3 million. In 1989 we will also take over responsibility for our buildings from the Property Services Agency, but extra monies will be provided accordingly.

Publications

The Galleries are committed to a very lively series of publications dealing especially with Scottish painting. Two years ago, with the sponsorship of the Scottish Post Office Board, we launched a series of inexpensive but scholarly little monographs on Scottish painters — called *Scottish Masters*. We now have published ten titles: William Aitkman, William Carrick, Alexander Carse, James Cox, Joan Eardley, Robert Herdman, John de Medina, Jacob More, James Tassie, and David Wilkie.

Buildings

Just as the National Museums are hoping to do, we are attempting to tell in a coherent way the history of Scotland, collecting especially the highpoints in artistic achievement. But we have three overcrowded buildings and none of them was designed or founded for this purpose. The original National Gallery building was conceived with a complex brief, one half of it was devoted to the National Gallery and the other half to the Royal Scottish Academy. It was only after 1910 that the Royal Scottish Academy moved out into what was the old Institution building on Princes Street, which allowed for the National Gallery to take over both sides of the present building. The National Portrait Gallery in Queen Street was purpose-built but is most unsuitable; with its huge windows looking onto Queen Street, it is a far from ideal space for showing portraits, in spite of what has been achieved recently with carefully conceived alterations and modifications. As for the National Gallery of Modern Art, it was designed as a school, not as a picture gallery at all. Many of us would love to have a huge custom-built gallery which would take over and look after the combined collections of the National Galleries, but we know this cannot be.

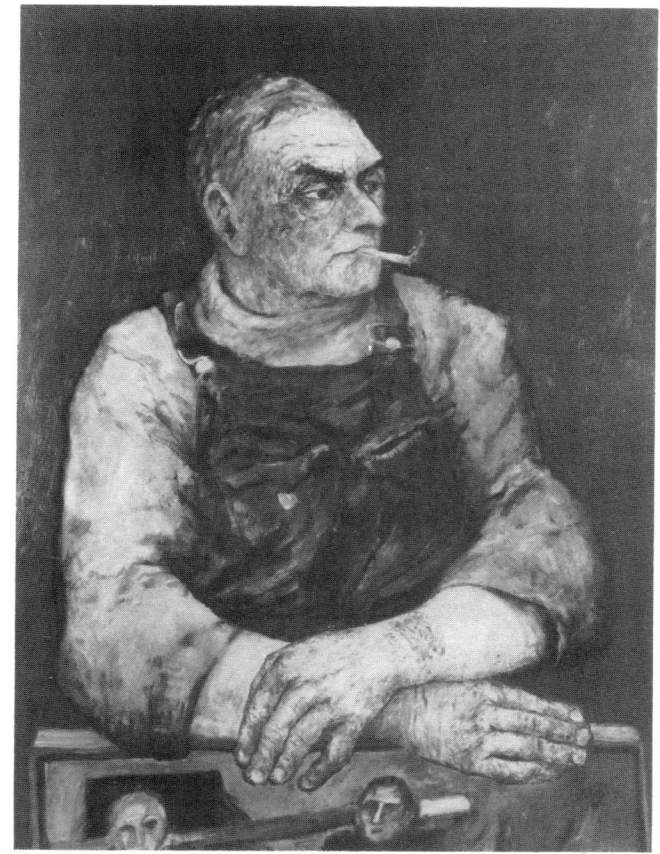

John Bellany: My Father.
Scottish National Gallery of Modern Art.

Just before I arrived in 1984 to take up the post of Director, the National Gallery of Modern Art opened. It works well; it is very nearly ideal, and it has a very lively acquisitions activity. It has a very good restaurant, easy parking, and the attendance figures are not too bad. At the National Portrait Gallery the interior renovation of the building is complete but the exterior is a headache. A recent report says that it will not be completed until 1991 or 1992 and it is going to cost about £2.5 million.

At the Mound we have now completed the redecoration of the National Gallery. Here we have a great piece of architecture in the centre of the capital city of Scotland on the one hand, and on the other we have a fine collection of pictures which we have to respect and interpret in the most lively and appropriate way we can. The foundation stone was laid in 1850 and the building, designed by Playfair, was mostly completed by 1857 although it was not opened until 1859. It is a fascinating building with twin porticos to north and south, those at the north-west and north-east were the original entrances to the Royal Scottish Academy and the National Gallery. The doors were subsequently converted to windows while the present central doorway was a tradesman's entrance and not a public space at all. A corridor ran down the middle of the building. It was a very nice tightly controlled little picture gallery, set in a marvellous Doric building next door to an elegant Ionic building with the General Assembly of the Church of Scotland looking splendidly perpendicular above, and the great mass of the castle rock louring over the whole thing. To have such an amazing group of distinguished buildings so close together is quite remarkable.

Playfair was arguably one of the finest architects that came out of 19th century Scotland. He designed the structure and employed David Ramsay Hay to devise the interior. Now David Ramsay Hay started as a simple painter doing marbling and graining and gilding. He was a prodigy of Sir Walter Scott and decorated for him the interiors of Abbotsford. From there he went on to greater things. This was a time in Scotland when objects were being carefully researched and all kinds of new ideas were issuing from the University of Edinburgh. Hay wrote a book on colour theory in 1828 and subsequently published many further articles on colour. Playfair worked in the closest possible relationship with Hay, 'the first intellectual house painter', who was responsible for redecorating the great Barry Room in the Royal Society of Arts in the Adelphi, London, and many of the interiors of the Palace of Holyrood House.

For the National Gallery his revolutionary colour scheme consisted of claret coloured walls, a Dutch weave carpet which was green, and the pedestals on which the sculpture stood were, truncated obelisks painted what might be described as geranium pink. The idea was that these two reds were intended to clash violently, invigorating and stimulating the eye. The red behind the pictures intensified their palette and the green foiled the activity of the two reds. The pictures were hung from floor to ceiling, the cornice was painted to look like oak, and the whole suite of rooms on both sides was connected by round-headed arches.

Now what we have tried to do at the National Gallery of Scotland is to respect the original as much as possible. We took down and preserved the 1938 columns and replaced the arches, working from the original Playfair drawings. We found splashes of red paint underneath the skirting showing the original colour and we restored the walls to match. We have purposefully chosen the correct red for the pedestals of the sculpture, and have laid an appropriate green carpet. The surviving pieces of Playfair furniture have been restored, and a firm in Edinburgh commissioned to make copies. We have rehung the paintings rather more sparsely, as we were not sure whether the public was ready for the density of a 19th century hang. In the room where the Raeburns are shown, for example, is the huge Wilkie we were given three years ago and there visitors will also see a marble bust of Wilkie which actually stood in that room in the 1860's.

As relief from the pompous parade spaces we have created a sort of 'kunstkammer', a little room devoted to highly finished pictures including the wonderful pair of Elsheimers painted on copper which you really need to examine closely. In this small gallery you get a really close view of the pictures and savour the feeling of their preciousness. We chose brown walls here, a colour which cannot interfere with one's appreciation of the beautiful paintings. We also laid a marble floor.

The other small octagon contains Poussin's *Seven Sacraments* and is entered from a grand Baroque space of French, Italian and Spanish pictures with sculpture and parade furniture underneath. The *Seven Sacraments,* which have been on long loan from the Duke of Sutherland, were shown upstairs in a room against coarse woven 'avocado' green tweed on the walls and grey pig's bristle carpet squares on the floor. The frames, which were in a poor state were beautifully regilded. Having decided to move the paintings to the small octagonal room we laid a marble floor copying one shown in Poussin's paintings. We produced a banquette for the middle of the room, because seating is essential, and copied it from the view of the triclinium in *The Sacrament of Penance* where Christ lies on just such a couch. Also copied from Poussin is the concept of the 'oil' lamp. It comes from the *Holy Eucharist.* The effect is that you are walking into a Poussin interior and seeing Poussins on the walls. In contrast to the parade rooms this space reminds one of a chapel devoted to private prayer, and you can contemplate in quietness these frozen sermons of the 17th century. These are pictures that you need to sit and contemplate quietly by yourself for they are not public images.

We cannot consider all the rooms in the National Gallery in detail but from the Poussins, as a complete break, we return to Holland in the 17th century. The furniture in this gallery is on loan to us from the National Museums of Scotland. We are most grateful to them for their generosity. The display case there is one of eight that we have had made copying those that existed originally in the National Gallery in the 19th century. These cases are going to be filled with Tassie medallions, and with miniatures from the National Portrait Gallery, with medals and plaquettes, and drawings. In the lower rooms, to the right and left, underneath the new floor which was put into the south end of the Gallery in 1971, grey walls remind one of Dutch 17th century interiors. They are highly flexible spaces where either paintings or drawings can be displayed the light levels being altered appropriately. Immediately behind it there is a new loading bay, and a new picture store which makes temporary exhibitions much easier to mount. The National Gallery has about 16,000 works on paper, so it is essential that we regularly have changing exhibitions of this material.

The visitor then into the Flemish 17th century room which can be seen from the Dutch 17th century room. Here can be enjoyed works by Van Dyck and Rubens. Part of Scotland's story is, of course, the story of when these paintings were acquired and why they were acquired. Some were extremely familiar to Wilkie and fellow artists of his generation. Several, including Van Dyck's *Lomellini Family,* were bought by Andrew Wilson, the Scottish landscape painter, who was in the 1830's domiciled in Genoa.

Upstairs the Modernist interiors have been swept away and been redecorated inserting skirting boards, chair rails, and cornices. Appropriate colours have been selected for the different periods of the pictures. We have also introduced furniture and sculpture. In particular on nearly every axis a picture has been hung which has Scottish connections. So, for example, the main picture in Room A2 is the wonderful painting of his second wife by Ramsay. The pink silk of the wall behind it was derived from Boucher's *The Assumption* and from the pink blush to the sky in the background of the other two Bouchers to the right and left, as well as the many other pinks which appear in all the 18th century pictures on the walls. *Mrs Bruce of Arnot,* for example, that other ravishing picture by Ramsay, is wearing a very similar pink. An attempt has not been made to reproduce an 18th century interior here, but we have attempted to produce a space in which one can see the pictures sympathetically. The blue room is next door, a room that has the painting by Raeburn of *Rev. Robert Walker skating*. It was first hung with tobacco coloured silk, which was beautiful in itself but hopeless as a foil to the pictures, for it was the most perfect camouflage you could wish to see; brown paintings against a brown wall. Then there is a wonderful vista through to the end room with

Benjamin West: Alexander III King of Scots saved from the fury of a stag by the intrepid intervention of Colin Fitzgerald. National Gallery of Scotland.

Sargent's portrait of *Lady Agnew of Lochnaw*. Again the background of that picture was the basis for the colour scheme here. These principles were followed in all the upstairs rooms including the Impressionist room. Here the colour has not been changed, only the texture of the walls. The colour is taken from the painted files that lie on the divan in that wonderful portrait by Degas of *Diego Martelli*. Downstairs you come to Scottish scenes by James Ward in the company of Turners and Constables, and then to the Scottish chieftains painted by Raeburn grouped appropriately in the final room which is dominated by the *Macdonell of Glengarry*. The huge picture by Benjamin West of *Alexander III King of Scots,* which we recently managed to acquire, came from the Town Hall of Fortrose, and originally was in Brahan Castle. It was bought by the National Gallery of Art Washington but its export was blocked and we subsequently acquired it. Downstairs we have the New Wing which was completed by 1976 which is filled with yet more Scottish art.

This is the briefest outline of some of the things we have been trying to do for Scottish art and art in Scotland at the National Gallery. What the Galleries have attempted to do all the time is to incorporate Scottish art with European art, for the best Scottish art and the best of European art blend together like a dream. Take, for example, that wonderful portrait by Ramsay of his wife which hangs between two pictures by Chardin. That hanging is deliberate and appropriate because Ramsay did not learn how to paint like that by staying in Scotland. He learnt to paint like that because he was in Rome. First of all he worked with Solimena and then he worked with Imperiali. When he was in Rome he obviously got to know well the French artists who were working at the Academy there. And you know you can almost confuse that picture with ones by Perronneau, Aved, and Tocque, for it is so very French. The scumbled way that the paint is handled in the background and the way the flowers are painted is so much like Chardin. It is not a coincidence I believe that Ramsay's son, the General, put together a wonderful collection of French 18th century pictures which formed the nucleus of the fine 18th century French pictures we have at the National Gallery in Scotland today.

When you return downstairs the continuity is maintained: you see the great Gavin Hamilton *Andromache bewailing the death of Hector*. This picture has been cleaned and relined and has a good frame on it now. It is put in a place of honour and hung amongst very splendid Italian and French and English pictures of the period. What one must bear in mind as far as Scotland is concerned, is that we mustn't be too inward-looking as Scots. This great picture by Gavin Hamilton was painted by a member of the Accademia Clementina at Bologna, a man who produced with Domenico Cunego 'Scola Italica Pictura', a man who had such an influence on European art that people like David and Ingres were strongly indebted to him. If we keep on acquiring works which are of consequence only to a Scottish public it would be short-sighted.

We are striving to continue to collect historic Scottish art and collect contemporary Scottish art. We want these pictures to be seen by a wider Scottish audience both in Edinburgh and elsewhere. We are interested in restoring our historic buildings while at the same time displaying our collections as well as we can to delight and entertain a very wide public.

Mary Queen of Scots Got Her Head Chopped Off – Anne Lacey as Mary, Alison Peebles as Elizabeth.

PRESENTING·SCOTLAND'S·STORY

THE DRAMA OF SCOTLAND'S HISTORY

Liz Lochhead

Liz Lochhead, poet and playwright, and Writer-in-Residence with the Royal Shakespeare Company. Her publications include: Grimsisters, 1981; Dreaming Frankenstein, 1984; True Confessions, 1985; and her plays include Blood and Ice; Now and Then; and Mary Queen of Scots got her head chopped off, with Communicado theatre company.

1. Mary Queen of Scots got her head chopped off
Country — Scotland: what like is it? It's a peat bog; it's a dark forest; it's a cauldron, a lie, a salt pan, a coal mine. If you're gie lucky it's a bright beer meadow or a park aukie, or maybe its a field of stains. It's a tenement or a merchant's hall. It's a whore house or a humble cot, Princes Street or Paddy's market. It's a fistful of fish or a pickle of oatmeal. It's a queen's banquet or roast meats and junkets. It depends, it depends. I dinna ken what like your Scotland is, here's mine.

National flower — the thistle. National pastime — nostalgia. National weather — smir, haar, drizzle, snow. National bird — the crow, the crowie, le corbeau moi.
'Voice like a choked laugh, rag baggle of bird in my black duds. All angles and elbows and broken oxter feathers, black beady een in my executioner's hood. No braw, but I think I hae a sort of black glamour. Do I no' put you in mind of a skating minister or the other foot the parish priest, the dirty beast. My nests are rickle of stickle. I live on lambs' eyes and road accidents. Oh see, after the battle man its a pure feast. My eyes are o'er big even for my belly. In lean years of peace, by belly thinks my throat's been cut.'

'Once upon a time, there were twa queens on the one green island. And the one green island was split into twa kingdoms, but no equal kingdoms. Naebody in their right mind would insist on that, for the northern kingdom was cold and small and the people were low statured and ignorant and fear'd of their lords, and poor. They were starving, and their queen was beautiful and tall and fair and frenchified. The other kingdom was large and prosperous with wheat and barley and fat kye in the fields o'er yeoman farmers and wool in their looms and beer in their barrels and at the mouth of her greatest river, a great port, a glistening city that sucked all wealth to its centre, which was a palace and a court of a queen. A queen who was a cousin, a clever cousin, a wee bit aulder and maybe no so braw as the other queen but a queen nevertheless. Queen o' a country wi' an army and a navy and a dominion over many lands. Twa queens, one green island, and ambassadors and courtiers came from many lands to seek their hands.'

That was an introductory speech from *Mary Queen of Scots Got Her Head Chopped Off* which I was lucky enough to work on with the Communicado Theatre Company. I don't really think I wrote the play so much as devised it with them. I wrote all the words, in the form in which they'll appear in the Penguin edition when it's published, but I devised the show very much with the company, the whole company.

I really do want to talk pretty anecdotally and very personally about my experiences in dramatising Scotland's story. I did say when I was invited to talk, that I would speak about working with Communicado but that I wasn't at all qualified. I think maybe a drama critic like Joyce McMillan might have been a good person to have along, to talk about the big sweep of Scottish theatre and the things that are going on in it. I'm afraid that I won't be able to give you that because I'm a biassed practitioner and I feel it's my duty to stay biassed so that I can practition.

So I'm going to talk about my gradual realisation that what I'm doing when I'm writing, either by omission or by commission, what I'm doing in common with all the other people who are writing plays in Scotland, is telling Scotland's story in dramatic form. I mean, whether it's John Byrne in *Tutti Frutti* or the Slab Boys, so absolutely brilliantly celebrating the mix of popular American culture and urban Scottish, especially urban Scottish machismo culture. I think he explores that culture, warts and all, with a great deal of irony and comment upon it. Or it's Chris Harren writing about the Glasgow rent strikes during the First World War, in the not totally sympathetic, uncompromising character of Elizabeth Gordon Quinn from his play of that name. This is a woman who rejects working class solidarity and politics, rejects their consolation with the line: 'I refuse to learn how to be poor' as she fights for a piano that she can't play anyway. Or Peter Arnott in *Losing Alec*. Peter Arnott in *Losing Alec* is writing brilliantly about the sour spirit. Literally the sour spirit is a ghost story about the sour spirit of male-dominated Glasgow labour party and trade union politics and how it has poisoned a marriage and blighted the development, both emotional, personal and cultural, of the next generation of his family. Or it's Marcella Evaristi, when she documents the precise family ironies and the double nationalities, the sense of being an exile from their own country, of a Scottish Italian middle-class family,where the mother dares to have an affair with a younger man. Evaristi in general, I think is very, very good on middle-class Scots. She has written a lot especially about middle-class Scottish girls growing up, a largely neglected area of Scottish drama.

Or, I think, of Tony Roper in *The Steamy,* his very popular play of 1987, a play about four women of different generations set in the 1950's on Hogmanay. In the Steamy with nothing very much happening they demonstrate to us, with the position of incredible dramatic irony which we have now, the hopes and fears and longings of Scottish women of that period shot through with the great songs of the group Wildcat which as part of that production gave it the kind of framework in which you could see these ironies. I think of Wildcat themselves, with their songs 'Welcome to Paradise','Heather up your Kilt', and 'The Painted Bird'. There are so many plays which have examined our Scotland in that mix of rock/theatre in music hall which is unique to them, and which, at its best, is brilliant, real, committed, go-for-it, biassed but admit it, agitprop. When they write things like 'Bed Pan Alley' to talk about the health service cuts or 'Dead Liberty' at the time of the miners' strike, it represents a certain kind of 'ad-hoc let's talk about it now' drama. Or if I think about the Daddy of them all, from my point of view, because I don't have a long culture in the theatre myself, I think of 'The Cheviot, The Stag and the Black, Black Oil' – John McGrath and 7:84 Theatre Company's play in the early seventies which was part of an enormous revival in epic theatre in Scotland. They managed to document the story of the clearances in a style that did include the epic and the popular and the vulgar and the committed with a lot of Brechtian influences and a lot of music hall. The play was full of gaelic songs and music of the most incredible haunting beauty and rage and magnificence. So this was a history and an entertainment put into the dramatic form, that was the form that they started off from and they burst the dramatic form apart to tell the peoples' experiences or their own history, their real own story.

Anyway, all these different things, I think, make up a mosaic. I don't think any one of us has the responsibility, thank God, of telling Scotland's story. I think if any of us tell the truth about our little bit of it, we should make it live, make it happen on the stage and get people in to look at it. Then all the different bits that are done by different people will surely add up to some sense of what Scottish culture was, and is, and will contribute to that picture and add to it rather than just commenting on what it has been so far. So it is this sense of realising what is your own story, and what bit you should talk about, that I want to talk about.

So, let's look at how *Mary Queen of Scots Got Her Head Chopped Off* came about. Communicado Theatre Company are a small touring theatre company who up until 1987 were only funded for single projects. They weren't revenue-funded from the Scottish Arts Council, although they were in good shape, and the Scottish Arts Council tended to look very sympathetically on their applications for funding for these single projects. But the difficulty, as can be imagined, of starting each project anew, was very considerable for a company without any base or administration.

The company only really existed in the mind of Gerry McGrew, the director, and other actors who always tend to form the nucleus of any Communicado piece. This company had been going during most of the 1980's and they took as their starting point one of their best starting productions, I think, an adaptation of *House with Green Shutters*. They tried to look at novels, often Scottish novels, and to find ways of dramatising them. Now they are a Scottish international company with influences, among others from Polish theatre.

Communicado is like that: none of us is expert on anything, but we know what we are doing in theatre and we grab our influences where we can. I think Gerry McGrew, Alison Peebles and Rob Picavan, who were the three founding members of Communicado, felt that they wanted to do popular touring theatre that was also challenging intellectually and was very visual in its theatricality. I would suggest however that, with my experience of working with them, they are actually a company who have a tremendous respect for text and the written word.

Mary Queen of Scots Got Her Head Chopped Off – Anne Lacey as Mary.

They had been going for about five years and had maybe six or seven productions. They had won about three or four Fringe Firsts, and they were regarded as being one of the first theatre companies in Scotland. Their administrator was unemployed and on social security but she was coming into a little borrowed office they had for the six months she and Gerry McGrew spent, with no money coming in at all, setting up the tour of Mary Queen of Scots. I felt slightly guilty because there was a mechanism for paying me. They had applied for a commission from the Arts Council and got me the money to write the play. I was doing my research and beginning to write while they were still completely supporting themselves while getting the project together. Now Gerry is as cynical as anybody else, in many ways. He knows that he must apply for funding all over the place. He knows that the Scottish Arts Council cannot be wholly responsible for funding things. More and more pressure is being put on all the Arts in Scotland to find sponsorship. Sponsorship can be a double-edged sword because, obviously, sponsors prefer to be attached to proven, tried and true, cultural artefacts. It is very, very difficult to get sponsorship for anything experimental or anything that you have not proved that you can do yet. Even with a good track record like Communicado, and writing I can't remember how many thousand letters for sponsorship were sent out. The sponsorship we managed to get together for the whole project was, I think, a ream of paper which was very well appreciated, and which printed the programmes. We also got a single bottle of Mary Queen of Scots champagne which didn't go round the whole company at the end of the first night. So, in their experience, actually applying for sponsorship cost them a lot of money.

When Gerry came through with the idea of Mary Queen of Scots, he said, 'we've got to do this because it's 1988 next year and it's the anniversary, it's the four-hundredth anniversary'. Of course, it turned out to be the four-hundredth anniversary of Mary Queen of Scots' *death* which says a lot to me about Scotland in the first place! That what we were going to celebrate was somebody getting their head cut off! However, that was one of the ironies which proved quite fertile once we began to work on the subject matter. Neither Gerry nor I knew a great deal about Mary Queen of Scots. I had once tried to plough my way through Antonia Fraser's exhaustive biography and got rather bored by it. So, it meant a lot of reading up but all we knew was that there was a powerful myth which is obviously a good core to start with in any drama. I don't mean myth in the sense of an untruth, I mean a myth in the sense of something which is so deeply and physically true for a whole nation that they have got to find a way of metaphorising it. Mary Queen of Scots had been a very handy metaphor for something that was obviously very powerful in the Scottish psyche.

When Gerry McGrew and I talked together we discovered our differences: Gerry, is an Irish Catholic Glaswegian Scot and I am not actually a Glaswegian at all. I was brought up not exactly in the country, but outside Motherwell, in a small village, a rural mining community. I was very much brought up as a Protestant Scot. Right from the start we found that, just by talking to each other, we could find quite a number of things that we wanted to say about this myth and that, therefore, if we could be honest about that we could be honest for quite a lot of Scotland. We already had a rural and an urban difference between us, and we had, obviously, a gender difference; we also had a religious difference and although we were more or less of the same class, I suppose, this meant that we had had completely different versions of the story told to us. Protestants are brought up in Scotland to believe that Mary Queen of Scots was a great threat to our wonderful reformation and if she had been allowed to live she might have brought down our revolution. Catholics, on the other hand, are brought up to believe that she was a martyr. In fact, there are often plans afoot in the Catholic church to make her a saint. So these two themes, the gender theme and the religious theme were very, very powerful themes to explore in terms of the story itself.

I found that everything I read became much more interesting. Antonia Fraser's book now suddenly, because I needed it, was a lot more useful, and it was a matter of finding out the basic core of the story and what I wanted this story to be. In the end, it became very much about Elizabeth and Mary, about two different women who were on two different thrones in the one island and how they solved the problem of being women, powerful women, rulers, or failed to solve these problems, in entirely different ways. Elizabeth prevailed by becoming a proxy man, and by refusing to marry, playing an interesting game. But then the irony was that by refusing to marry and produce an heir (which would have put her in danger), she made it clear that her achievements were doomed to be infertile and would die with her. So we began to explore this story in terms of power: to reduce it to its forces. I developed the argument between Knox and Mary, for instance. We decided that we wanted one dancer and one musician – we only had six actors – and we also decided that we really didn't want to do the kind of 'theatre and education' bit with everybody rushing on stage in different hats and different costumes playing the parts of casts of thousands.

I am aware that this is not going to be very popular with historians, but we felt that our duty was not to the details of historical accuracy as it would be if we were mounting a museum display or trying to tell a history. We were making a drama exploring the underlying forces existing at that time in Scotland, and doing that as truthfully as we could.

This reduction of the story to its essential forces also made it possible to tell it with our small cast of six actors, one dancer and one musician. For the wedding of Darnley and Mary, for example, we had to invent a wedding ceremony. The company looked like a pack of ragged, fairground people, their costumes were quite dirty and ragged and tattered under the armpits. We wanted them to look rough and dirty and as they appeared on stage, just after the speech that I read at the beginning of this chapter, the audience gradually learned who they were. Each actor played one character, but they also played multiple other nameless characters anytime we needed them. Mary herself was played by Ann Lacey who has a wonderful mediaeval face.

Here is an example of the argument. Mary says to Knox, 'Mr Knox, I see in you yen who is convinced he be moved by love of God but is in truth fired rather by hatred o' mankind'.

Knox: 'There is yen a boon as a' madam, who is the best judge, the only. You raised up a part of this nation, ma subjects against ma mother and against me their prince, anointed by God. You hae written a treasonous tritae of a book against ma just authority. You have been the cause of great sadition and greater slaughter in England. I profess the right worshipin' o' God and by the right worshipin' o' God, men learn from their hearts to obey their just princes. But you think I hae nae just authority. You majesty if this realm finds no inconveniency in the regiment o' women than that which they approve shall I not futher disallow.
Mary: Except within your own heart and breast my heart is God's but I shall be as well content to live under yea as Paul was to live under Nero. Say you will gie to Ceasarina what Ceasarina's.
Knox: I see madam kens her scriptures.
Mary: I ken ma scriptures. I hae bathe heard and read. Mr Knox, because I am by nature doose and quiet dinna think I hae nae convictions nor believes locked in ma silent heart, though I dae not trumpet them abroad.
Knox: Well if I did blow the first blast of the trumpet, madam, against the monsterous regiment o' women, this blast was neither against your person or your regiment, but against that bloody jesibel o' England. etc.

Here is La Corbie speaking to Mary just after this. She says: 'gin yae want to gag Mr Knox you will hae to abolish the mass and embrase his cold kirk'.
Mary: 'And, is there nae comfort in his kirk?'

La Corbie: 'Aye, cold comfort, but there are those who sae all the better suits the climate.'
Mary: 'And yae think ginna sat on St Giles' hard pews on a Sunday, I'd sit surer on ma ane throne all week lang'.
La Corbie: 'Nae dou't about that. He has couped the queen o' heaven so how should he worry o' couping a mere earthly queen?'
Mary: 'Then the protistants dinna love our blessed virgin?'
La Corbie: 'Knox has torn the mother of god from out the sky of Scotland and has tramped her celestial blue gown among the muck and mier and has blotted out every name by which ye praise her. Stella Maris, Star of the Sea, Holy Mother, Notre Dame, Our Lady of Perpetual Succour.'
Mary: 'But if he had torn her fro' the blue sky what has he left in her place?'
La Corbie: 'A black hole, a jagged gash, naethin''.
Mary: 'But how should I live without Our Lady?'
La Corbie: 'Easy. You hae lived without yer earthly mother so you can live without yer heavenly yin.'
Mary: 'I will marry who I can love'.
And that was the central crux and argument of it. The exciting discovery we made while doing the play was that we wanted to do it in Scots or in a sort of Scots — a new invented Scots. I had always thought that I was someone who spoke with a strong Glaswegian accent but wrote in English. I must say its been an incredible revelation: to be building up a mosaic of modern urban Scots and the old language that Knox wrote his arguments in. Put together they formed a single whole, as if we were working from a single united spirit which is, I think, what we were very much doing in this production.

2. Heritage Culture
I would like to end this paper with a different subject altogether, a bit of agit. prop. cabaret on the subject of Scottish 'heritage culture'.

'Hello, hello, hello. My name's Vicky and I'm your waitress for this evening. And tonight's specials are the Tagliatelle King Billy — that's a generous portion

Mary Queen of Scots Got Her Head Chopped Off – Stuart Hepburn (Bothwell), Anne Lacey (Mary).

of the Pasta Place's blue pasta (that's real pasta, fresh pasta); a scrumptious swill of scarlet al sugo tomato sauce, a white sauce made with wine, cream and garlic and a dollop of blue cheese on top. We also do a Parkhead Centenary Bake — that's spinach and white fish in alternate Celtic stripes. You see, apparently Morris thinks that Sectarianism is coming back into fashion as a fun thing. Could be, you know. Morris is seldom wrong. He's usually got his finger right on the pulse.
I mean take this place. Do you's like this place? Well, I suppose you's must. I mean, you've had to queue for very nearly an hour and half trying to get in. And unless this is your first time here and you're only trying to be trendy, you've actually liked it well enough to come back. Well there's no accounting for taste. I mean, if I didn't work here, I wouldn't be seen dead in the place. You see, I happen to know what goes on behind those swing doors in that kitchen but, och well, it's flavour of the month and the tips are brilliant so who's complaining?

Do you like the decor? I think that's Morris' forte really. I mean, that plus the ambiance. I mean, him and Gregor, that's Morris' boyfriend and business partner, they fought over this place something terrible but I told them all along that I thought that 'The Hungry Thirties' was a fabulous name for a restaurant. I mean, you want to attract the older crowd. I mean, that's where all the money is these days. Not that all our clientele are over thirty, of course. Far from it, but Hungry Over Twenty-Fives just doesn't have that same sort of a sloaney tone to it, does it? Oh, we've got them as well you know. Glasgow's no different.

I mean, we got a good write up, you know, in the *Glasgow Herald's* 'Trendy Man's Food Column'. I mean, he slagged the food of course but he waxed absolutely lyrical about the waiters with their galoshes, cordless grampes simits, big tweed bunnets and hob-nailed miner's boots. Plus us waitresses with our neatly rolled hair, cross-over pinnies and, a lovely wee touch this is I think, stockings rolled down to the ankles, and Ma Broon's slippers.
So the write up did help and you know, now in here on a Saturday night, you know, you'll not get a table for love nor money. Not in 'The Hungry Thirties'. Well, not for money anyway but if you happen to be a guy of a certain build and you catch Morris's eye when Gregory isn't looking, then a table might just be found for you.

Och, I quite like it really. Apart from some of the other staff, that is. You see, I am a professional waitress unlike some. MA History and Politics from Glasgow University, two years in the ???????. No I am not an actress actually. Jesus-H-Christ! Ever since Bill Forsyth discovered queer C P Grogan in the spaghetti factory ma heart has been absolutely roasting with all the real egits I get working at the next station to me. I mean, can't carry more than about 3 plates at a time, and skiting about the floor, spilling Gazpacho down the back of some poor guy's brand new Martinique shirt. Pathetic! And, I mean, always asking for a lunchtime off or to change their shift, 'to go up and see if my agent's got anything' or to go for an interview. No. No they don't call it an audition these days. No. No, apparently, it's only adoring mothers with red patent tap shoes in their handbag taking Lena Zavarone Mark II up to the Maryhill Hall for the touring festival of Amazing Technicolour Jesus Christ Cats Superstar that actually call it an audition. This lot call it an interview. Not that they ever get the job. Nor are they quite all there in this job either. I mean, the only time they ever spring to life is when some guy from the BBC comes in. Then they are practically down on all fours under the table fighting to be one to serve him his 'Kippers Kier Hardy' or 'Mince & Potatoes John McLean'.

So this is definitely the business to be in in Glasgow these days, isn't it? Hospitality and Catering. I mean, the Licensed Trade's Veterans and Restaurantuers Association are blessing the day the bloody Burrell Collection thing opened it's door. Christ knows where it is. Over in the south side somewhere. I mean, no bugger can find it anyway, I'll tell you that. I mean, just picture all our tourists. Oh we have got them as well you know. Glasgow's no different. I mean, just picture all our tourists in their BMWs Burrell-bound, getting lost on the motorway, looping the loop on the Kingston Bridge and just generally giving up and taking the next exit off and going for something to drink and something to eat instead. So, well, what with the Garden Festival and Ninety Ninety and The Year of Culture and The Opera and The Mackintosh and everything like that, well I think it will be really brilliant to see all those welders and riveters of yesteryear becoming the waiters of tomorrow. Well, they couldn't not be any worse than those bloody actors.'

Speed bonnie boat like a bird on the wing, | Carry the lad that's born to be king,
Onward the sailors cry; | Over the seas to Skye.

Speed Bonnie Boat.

DE-PICTING SCOTLAND: FILM, MYTH AND SCOTLAND'S STORY

John Caughie

John Caughie is senior lecturer in Theatre, Film and Television Studies at Glasgow University and co-director of the John Logie Baird Centre for research on television and film. He was one of the organisers of the Scotch Reels event at the Edinburgh Film Festival in 1982 and has published widely.

There is a scene in the Hollywood musical *Brigadoon* in which the eighteenth-century Highland village dominie interrupts tending his kailyard to explain to two very twentieth-century New Yorkers (Gene Kelly and Van Johnson) how it came to be that the village into which they have stumbled suffered its miraculous arrested development. In a period which can be dated by internal textual evidence to the years immediately preceding Culloden, the Highlands of Scotland were threatened by roving bands of evil witches who tempted the people from the traditional ways (a wonderfully blatant example of 'blaming the victim' which displaces onto the disadvantaged everything from Cumberland's army, through Patrick Sellar, to the oil industry and fish farming). In order to protect his flock, the minister of Brigadoon, Mr Forsyth (a family name that echoes down the centuries) did a deal with God that the village would be put into a deep sleep, waking only for one day every hundred years. 'In this way', says the dominie, with all the innocence of the kailyard 'we would never be in any century for long enough to be touched by it.'

Though Murray Grigor has suggested that *Brigadoon* might be a Scottish documentary, historians seem to agree that there is no convincing evidence for the village's historical existence and archaeologists have found no conclusive traces (though this may have been because they were looking on the wrong day). While the possibility of a Brigadoon Theme Park or a Heritage Centre offers exciting opportunities for enterprise, in the absence of a Museum of Brigadoon exhibiting authentic artefacts we have to conclude that the village only exists in the archaeology of the Scottish imagination, concealed for ever and its day in the mists of the various imaginary Scotlands which many of us from time to time inhabit.

Now I have never been entirely taken in by the myth of Brigadoon, though I have from time to time identified strongly with Harry Seton, the character in the film who tries unsuccessfully to cross the bridge which separates the miraculous timelessness of the village from real, historical time (he is killed trying to escape); and I am sometimes brought up short by the startled realization that the tartan monster is still alive and roaming the land (possibly disguised in the new tartan uniforms of the custodians of Historic Buildings). But neither am I entirely taken in by the mythology of authentic objects, or the claims that original materials are the exclusive repositories of a true national past. What I want to argue is that the defining mythologies of a society, the imaginary constructs by which it defines and recognises itself, are as material as its butter churns or its lobster creels. These mythologies cannot simply be construed as false consciousness to be corrected by hard facts and things you can put in display cabinets. They have material effects, positive and negative, and while they may have oblique relationships to national histories, they are probably foundational for national memories. The tartan myth of Brigadoon, the triumphal defeatism of Culloden, the couthy community of the kailyard are both massively regressive and, at the same time, provide some of the images by which Scottish people recognise and misrecognise themselves and insist on some kind of nationality.

It's in this context that, while recognising the critical importance of 'doing history', I also want to argue for the value of 'doing mythology', and using representations — films, television programmes, postcards: the ways we are represented or represent ourselves — to do it. It is often in the gap between history and representations, in seeing what is not represented in popular discourses, as well as what is represented and how it is represented, that the understanding of the experience of a time and a place lies. The evidence isn't either in myth or in documented history, but in the exchange between them. It's in that sense that I want to argue that film, popular feature film, and television may constitute, if not authentic objects, at least a source of complementary evidence which museums could well incorporate into their recovery of the past.

Scotland and Scotland's story

A story is a way of ordering events into a progressive narrative with a beginning a middle and an end, even if, as Jean-Luc Godard says, it is not always necessarily in that order. Linear history, one damn thing after another, constructs progression, ordering the meaning of the past at the expense of its real disorder. That kind of history, the story of the past, seeks out the rationalities of causes and effects, bundling the irrationalities into inconsequentiality and historical accident.

Poster illustrating Scotch Myths, an exhibition originated by the Crawford Centre for the Arts, St Andrews.

The defining myths of a society seem to cut across that rational movement, freezing time into a punctual moment, a point of return which is continually present in the national imaginary, providing the images by which we are invited to recognise ourselves. The points at which these defining myths intersect with historical progression are points of rupture, conflict, transformation.

Think of the Western. Behind the gunfights at the OK Corral and the stranger riding in out of the desert, there are real and historic social, economic and political tensions around the building of frontier communities: conflicts between a stable and a nomadic society, between settlement and free range agrarian economies. According to Frederick Jackson Turner in his 'Turner Thesis'[1], developed at the end of the nineteenth century and still influential in more recent historical writing, it is the presence of this frontier and the tensions and social forms associated with it which explains subsequent American social and political development. This is the moment which the myth of the Western returns to, resolving its real contradictions in stories, and plundering it for images of the nation. Its continuing resonance can be heard in the rhetoric of the various 'New Frontiers'. Culloden provides just such a moment, though in a much less affirmative way, for the final construction of the British state, the taming of the last wilderness.

The interest for historiography of film and popular representations is not to uncover the past as it really was but to discover it as it was, and continues to be, imagined. An archaeology (in Foucault's sense[2]) of the social imaginary takes as its 'documents' not just the potshards and authentic objects but also the various discourses, illegitimate as well as legitimate, which have at varying times been used to make sense of these historical facts. Rather than using authentic objects to immunize people from the falsifications of popular representations, we could recognize that these are the myths that people carry around with them as cultural baggage. Museums could be in the business of unpacking that baggage, and if that were part of the project, then film could be useful material.

Scotland seems to be quite distinctive in the centrality which mythologies occupy in its sense of a national past and a national identity: perhaps a token of an inferiorism which seeks the reassurance of an epic rather than a 'real' past, or perhaps, indeed, a function of its status as the frontier of Europe in the age of Romanticism. From popular as well as legitimate cultural representations, three immediately recognisable Scottish myths seem to emerge: these can be identified as 'Tartanry', 'Kailyard' and 'Clydeside'.

Tartanry
'Tartanry' the most obvious, the most notorious and, in its tourist manifestations, the most embarrassing, takes Culloden as its privileged moment, with a wider reference to the eradication of an historically anachronistic and economically unproductive feudal system and its replacement with a relatively productive free range agrarian system which provided raw material, timber and fleece, for the factories of the emerging industrial revolution, and, later, provided recreation for the people who profited from the factories. Economically, the epic transformation is tied to the industrial revolution. Culturally, it is tied to the Romanticism which sought wildness in the now empty landscapes of one of the last wildernesses of Europe, emptied by Cumberland and the Clearances, and filled, by Scott and MacPherson, with wild, charismatic men and elusive, fey women. Almost invisible behind the tartan monster which stalks airport terminals, High Street souvenir shops, and Hollywood movies, are real mythic confrontations between progress and tradition, nature and culture, rationality and romance. While many of us would stand back quite happily and watch, from our 'distant distinction', the tartan babies being thrown out with the bath water, there is something in that powerful confrontation, in the complicated appeal of land and landscape, which seems written into Scottish culture, and which needs to be recognised and understood.

The Fresh Air Fortnight.

Kailyard

If Culloden is the privileged moment of Tartanry, the privileged moment of the Kailyard mythology must be 1843, the Great Disruption of the Church of Scotland, and division within the stable communities of the small townships. Of less epic resonance than the clash of nature and culture embodied by images of Romantic wildness, the imagery and imaginary of the Kailyard is domesticated and social, concerned with the disturbance in manners caused by religious divisions, divisions which had real social consequences, but which are moderated by the couthy and benign view from the manse window. The kailyard passes into popular culture most famously or notoriously through Harry Lauder, though he was only more consciously comic than J. M. Barrie who had been every bit as popular on the American lecture circuit only a few decades earlier. *The Little Minister* was adapted three times by the Hollywood film industry before 1940. Today, the kailyard finds its natural home in the publications of D. C. Thomson, and on television with the excesses of Lauderism only gradually being squeezed out of Hogmanay to find a more innocuous form in a regional soap opera, *Take The High Road* which inherits the couthy mantle of the long-remembered Tannochbrae[3]. Less aggressive than tartanry, the Kailyard may be every bit as stifling, though there is no reason why it should not also echo with the real divisions in the community which first gave it life.

Clydesideism

'Clydesideism' is the mythology of the Scottish twentieth century, the one which seems currently most potent, and least acknowledged as mythology. The gritty realism of urban life parades itself as the modernised antidote to all those legends of tartanry and couthy tales of kailyard, but it is only the mythology of male industrial labour, with its appurtenances of pub and football field alive and in place, supporting the celebration of a 'real Glasgow' beneath the yuppie surface of shopping malls and Garden Festivals and Cities of Culture. As real 'productive' industrial labour ('the masculine domain') disappears into consumption ('the feminine domain'), the myth becomes more desperate.

Each of these mythological frameworks, then, takes its reference from a real transformative moment in Scottish history: the break-up of the clan system, and the taming of the wilderness in the eighteenth century; the Great Disruption in the Church of Scotland, and the resulting shifts within the community in the nineteenth century; and the rise and fall of industrial manufacturing in the twentieth century. As a way of understanding history, these seem to offer points of orientation, giving a sense of how the story seems to be organised. They are also the points of return for both popular and legitimated culture. Museums might use them as material for investigation, and, in these contexts, film, television and other contemporary popular representations become the evidence and the artefacts which need to be placed.

As a point of departure, there seem to me to be two points of interest for constructing Scotland's story. The first is that each of the myths has its negation, an underside which contests the familiar and acceptable images. Thus the romance of nature and of wild epic conflict are negated by the desolation of

Frae a Frien' o' Thine.

the Clearances and by the organised political and economic conflict of the Crofters' Wars; the benign parish community of the Kailyard is negated by the patriarchal sexual repression of *Gillespie*[4] or *The House with Green Shutters*[5]; and the celebration of male industrial labour with all its symbolic and unsymbolic violence is negated by the absence of women who are routinely idealized, victimized or forgotten. Within the mythology, within the popular discourses about Scotland, each of these negations is met with a silence. There is no film I know about the Clearances; no-one to my knowledge has ever adapted the eminently televisable *Gillespie;* and feature films and television plays are still about boys' games. Clearly this is first of all a problem for film and television. But is there a way for museums to address those silences, or will it be left to the heritage industry working with historians?

Secondly, the cross-cultural references of the mythology seem to offer rich ground for comparative exhibitions. Scotland as the frontier territory of Europe, romanticised as the last wilderness in art, music and literature, begs for comparison with the American West idealised as epic ground in popular fiction and film: the cattle markets of Crieff and Abilene, frontier towns marked out in equal degree by lawlessness; the wild clansmen and the native Americans mythologised as noble and not so noble savages; the conflict between settlement and free range fought out in the Cattle Wars of late nineteenth century America and in the Clearances and Crofters' Wars of late nineteenth Scotland. And, for the twentieth century urban myth, something of the mythology of Chicago, best represented in the thirties Gangster movie, echoes in the urban mythology of the Glasgow gangs of the twenties and thirties and in sectarian violence since then. In both versions of the myth, two waves of immigration confront each other. In Chicago, the Irish come first and colonise law and local government. The Italians, or the Sicilians, come next and take up their position outside the law. In Glasgow, the Highlanders come first and become, in the stereotype, bobbies and skilled labour in heavy industry; the Irish come next and are represented as navvies and washerwomen. A conflict of employment, but also of religion: unlike the Chicago of the Gangster movie, in the Glasgow version there is no priest to hold the jacket for both sides. The Gangster movie and the celebration of street fighting men play out as story the real conflicts of urban immigration, of rural immigrants becoming citizens, in the same way as the Western and the romance of the Highlands play out the historic conflicts of rural settlement and development. One of the ways of understanding these epic moments for museums might be by looking at the similarities and differences in the ways in which they have been placed in their specific and different histories.

So, I am arguing for museums to take on the mythologies which inform popular perceptions of the 'true history' which they exhibit, neither consigning them to false consciousness, nor seeking to stamp them out by a course of innoculative (and probably innocuous) treatment. This means using the postcards and the biscuit tins as Murray and Barbara Grigor have done. It also means using film and television material in a critical way, and it may mean calling on others for help and participation. In this sense, I suppose I am also arguing for museums to have a point of view.

This may be contentious. But what seems utterly uncontentious to me, and what seems blindingly obvious, is that for many museums the presence of a Scottish Film Archive offers a resource which has been unaccountably ignored. Even the purest defender of the true artefact must recognise that film, and, increasingly, televison offer a record of twentieth century life which no other generation has had.

Film as archive, then, as well as film as a repository of popular and defining mythology can not be disregarded. The French painter, Paul Delaroche, when he saw his first daguerreotype in 1839 is reputed to have said. 'From today, painting is dead.' He was a little premature, of course, but he was right to recognise that the presence of photography was going to change notions of representation. I have a fantasy of a museum director looking at film or television, archive or not, and saying, 'From today, boring displays of the life of the past are dead.'

Footnotes
1. Frederick Jackson Turner, 'The significance of the frontier in American history', paper given to the American Historical Association in 1893. Collected in Everett E. Edwards (ed.) *The Early Writings of Frederick Jackson Turner,* Madison, 1938. See also Henry Nash Smith, *Virgin Land: the American West as Symbol and Myth,* Harvard UP, 1950.
2. Michel Foucault, *The Archaeology of Knowledge,* Tavistock, 1972.
3. BBC: *Dr Finlay's Casebook.*
4. *Gillespie,* John Macdougal Hay (1914).
5. *The House with the Green Shutters,* George Douglas (1901).